The Ultimate
Practice Adjustment

Chris Tomshack DC

First published by Dog Ear Publishing
4010 W. 86th Street, Ste H
Indianapolis, IN 46268
www.dogearpublishing.net

ISBN: 978-1-4575-2657-2

This book is printed on acid-free paper.

Printed in the United States of America

Foreword

Over the past ten years, I have had the privilege of speaking to tens of thousands of chiropractors in many different countries. I have spoken at state, provincial, national, and international chiropractic association meetings. I have spoken for research foundations and chiropractic colleges. I have taught the postgraduate modules for the Wellness Lifestyle Program I developed for the International Chiropractors Association, and I have presented at countless other chiropractic events. I have also spoken at many chiropractic coaching seminars as a guest keynote speaker.

I was recently asked by a group of chiropractic leaders to provide what I consider to be the most important single concept or message that I teach. I will share with you what I shared with them. The most important thing anyone who serves patients will ever do is make the following distinction. You do not get paid and make a living from selling the services or interventions you offer. You get paid and make a living from the outcomes your services and interventions elicit for the patient. This is not a mere semantic distinction; it is the foundation of ethical practice, financial success, and patient satisfaction. Achieving the best possible patient outcomes is the cause of all practice success; the ethical-doctor income that results is simply the effect of consistently eliciting phenomenal patient outcomes.

As I have traveled around the chiropractic community for the past decade, I have often been seen as an outlier. I have always wondered aloud, often *very* aloud, why chiropractic-practice "gurus" were teaching the importance of tracking new patient numbers, average patient visit numbers, and average patient revenue numbers but were not teaching the importance of tracking the most important statistic in any healthcare practice: **Patient Outcome Average**. Who cares how many people you get through the door, how many times they come, or how much money they spend if they are not getting phenomenal outcomes?

In order to track patient outcomes, you have to have valid outcome measures. Perhaps this has been the biggest problem of all. If the foundation of practice success is patient outcomes, then the foundation of patient outcomes is valid patient assessment and clinical protocols. A successful practice must be able to assess the state of the patient, apply the required interventions to restore and maintain health and function, and track patient outcomes and progress (benefits of care) throughout the *entire* doctor-patient relationship.

What this all really means is that the doctor must be able to answer what I have called the three most important questions in healthcare: (1) What is the patient's current state of health or sickness; what is the patient's current health risk status? (2) Why is the patient in their current state; what is the *cause* of the state of health or sickness the patient is currently in? (3) What is required to get *and keep* this patient well; what interventions and advice are required to allow this patient's mind and body to return to a state of health and function?

About a year ago, something extraordinary happened: I ceased to be an outlier. I met Dr. Chris Tomshack, and in him, I found someone who felt as strongly about the importance of making patient outcomes the foundation of practice success as I do. I met someone who was not only willing to speak about this core value but who was willing to act upon it and implement whatever was necessary to help doctors achieve it.

My areas of expertise are evidence-based assessments and interventions to produce the best patient outcomes. I am a *patient*-management guru; I am a *patient-outcomes* guru. Dr. Tomshack's expertise is in the development of practice models and systems to deliver the best possible assessments and interventions to patients. Dr. Tomshack is always looking for ways to maximize practice success in a model that maximizes patient outcomes and the ethical-doctor income that naturally flows as a result. Dr. Tomshack is in the business of teaching doctors how to make a living from the outcomes they elicit from patients.

The era of doctor-centered, false claim-based chiropractic- and therapy-based diagnosis and treatment is over. The era of patient-outcome-centered, evidence-based, chiropractic- and lifestyle-based wellness and prevention has arrived. The era of addressing the cause rather than treating the effect is here. It is the only viable solution. It is the most scientific solution. It is the most evidence-based solution. Most importantly, it is the most effective solution to maximize patient outcomes for health and function. It is, and has always been, the chiropractic solution.

I am both pleased and proud to say that, as a result of our shared core values regarding the central importance of patient outcomes as the foundation of practice success, Dr. Tomshack and I are now working hard to discover ways for HealthSource to make the best use of my expertise. I firmly believe that, with the combination of the evidence-based assessments and intervention protocols that I have developed and the HealthSource practice systems model that Dr. Tomshack has developed, we have the ability to create the most successful doctors, eliciting the best health-patient outcomes that the world has ever seen. That is not hyperbole; this is an expected outcome that we have both independently been working toward for years. We are now finding ways to work synergistically, and the possibilities are quickly unfolding.

I congratulate Dr. Tomshack on his book, but most of all, I congratulate him for his devotion to put patient outcomes first and to create a model of practice success built upon this foundation.

Read this book, consume and digest its ideas, and take action to be the best doctor you can be.

—Dr. James L. Chestnut, BEd, MSc, DC, CCWP

Acknowledgments

My main purpose in writing this book was to simply share the truths necessary in achieving practice success in today's environment. What you do with this information is entirely up to you. My quest for knowledge and truth has been a lifelong endeavor, and it will never end. My hope is that you join me on this quest for truth. This quest sets the stage for a fantastic life.

Achieving success is not a solitary journey. Many people have helped me immensely, and I am eternally grateful for both their wisdom and their ability to share it with me. In particular, I'd like to express my gratitude to the following people.

Rob Berkley, whose wisdom is unparalleled.

Bob Campana, who has taught me more about win-win than I ever would have imagined was possible.

Brian Dugger, whose quest for personal development is a shining light in my life. We push each other endlessly, and it makes us better people and better leaders.

Jim Hoven, DC, and Dav Neubauer, DC, whose exemplary character always brightens my day.

Frank Dachtler, Steve Szucs, Kristen Wallace, Jenn Work-Smith, Jennifer Gandee, Amy DeFilippo, Jenna Porostosky, Caitlin Lima, Robbie Summers, Amber Turman, and Adam Horwitz, whose tireless dedication to the HealthSource family inspires me.

Dr. BJ Palmer, whose mission to develop chiropractic while continuously searching for better outcomes is the model on which HealthSource is built.

My "Elite Mastermind." These guys have incredible talent and have helped germinate more ideas in my mind than can be quantified.

My Regional Developers. This is an amazing team that relentlessly spreads the HealthSource mission.

Our huge family of HealthSource franchise owners. They all inspire me every day to do my absolute best and never settle for "good enough." They are why HealthSource exists.

My parents, whose unconditional love laid the framework for who I am today. I am eternally indebted to my absolutely incredible and loving mom and my late father, who was my best friend and the wisest person I've ever met.

My awesome kids, Shannon, Chris, and Zack, whose own journeys I watch unfold with utter amazement.

And my bride, Lisa, who is the love of my life and loves me in spite of my often unbalanced and manic drive. She inspires me with unconditional love!

Contents

CHAPTER 1

Who Changed the Rules and Didn't Tell Me?

"It's what you learn after you know it all that really matters."

—John Wooden

This book will have maximum impact if it is being read by a chiropractor, chiropractic spouse, or chiropractic student. If you are not one of these three types of individuals, you can still gain an enormous amount from reading and using the information contained herein, since the principles are universal. Let's go to work!

Unless your head has been under a rock for the past several years, you've noticed that someone changed the rules on how to be successful in chiropractic practice today. It's a totally different arena than that which existed just several years ago, and the rules will continue to change at breakneck speed. Those who are aware of these ongoing changes and know how to work with them instead of against them will prosper. Those who are ignorant of the changes will suffer greatly. Since you've chosen to read this book, you're likely in the former group rather than the latter. That's good!

Briefly, at least for now, suffice it to say that the rules have changed concerning the following areas: attracting more new patients, attracting more referral new patients, keeping compliant documentation, generating fair compensation for your services, having exit strategies, dealing with insurance hassles, running compliant cash-based practices, and creating a practice that allows the doctor to have success and freedom.

What worked in the 1990s is now woefully inefficient and non-compliant and will likely cause you to go broke in today's environment. Fast-forward to the years 2002 to 2013 and it's pretty much just as depressing. Change is either good, bad, or indifferent. The changes we are seeing now, while although damaging to most chiropractic practices, are actually good in the long run. It's similar to what happens following a forest fire. Immediately following the blaze, nothing is apparent but the sight of scorched earth and barren ground. Just a few short days following the fire, however, the first signs of new life and healthy growth begin to show themselves. What was once black and barren is almost magically transformed to a beautiful green, indicating the promise of growth to come. At first blush, this idea may seem counterintuitive, but it will make sense as you dive deeper into this book, so please, keep an open mind and be certain that you *CAN* build an amazing practice and lifestyle in today's age.

So what's going on? You could ask one of the gurus in our profession for their opinion, but they're pretty hard to find these days. In years past, all you had to do was open any one of our chiropractic magazines and newspapers and find them literally filled with full-page advertisements by practice-management coaches and gurus. Today, that's all different. You see, a Guru is someone with a particular skill. Today, that is insufficient. Practice is much more complicated now. A Mentor, on the other hand, possesses a wide skill set that he or she can deploy with you to work with you as you and your clinic grow over the long haul.

As running a successful practice has become more complicated than mastering a particular skill, we've seen many of the gurus resort to selling their clients the latest piece of equipment or gadget or internet marketing kit in the hopes of continuing to attract clients. You should steer clear of this in a major way. Mentorship is the answer, either by an individual (very rare) or by a highly competent group.

I'm not trying to slam gurus, because many of these people had phenomenal practices and did an enormous amount of good for patients and even for some of the doctors they coached, but the environment in which they built those practices was *completely* different then what is present today. In short, if you want to build a practice like those that thrived in the environment of the 1980s, 1990s, or even 2000s, you are in for a very stressful and unrewarding practice life.

If you're like me, I love to flip through the chiropractic trade journals in the hope that I can find something of interest, something that can truly help chiropractors succeed in today's challenging environment. I call this environment the New Profession. In today's New Profession, many of those who used to teach no longer do. There are many reasons for this, but the common factor is that doing things now is different. In some cases, compared to the "old days," it can be hard, very hard, to get the results that practice-management gurus taught. Why, you ask? The reason for this shift in building a successful practice is found in the New Profession itself. Although some of the basics of building a great and thriving practice are the same as they were when BJ was in his prime, much has changed.

Frankly, it's been quite tough identifying the new rules and then testing and proving systems to allow a DC to thrive in the new rules. Most solo DCs are finding it very hard or nearly impossible to learn all this on their own without the benefit of great mentorship. Case in point, let me describe a recent chiropractic trade show I attended. I packed up some of Team HealthSource, and off we went to attend the large chiropractic event and man a booth there. We'd had a booth there for the past four or five years. This year was markedly different. Attendance seemed way down. Enthusiasm was certainly down. The number of vendors was greatly reduced. It was as if a spirit of apathy was present, and that's a shame, because there is no need for apathy in our great profession. What is needed is ethical and sound systems to implement in your practice so you can compliantly have a blast.

At this event, the doctors and their teams did not have the usual zest and energy. They seemed preoccupied, and that's a shame because good information was being presented. The doctors and their teams were preoccupied due to the changes of the New Profession and the simple fact that they did not know what to do next.

It harkens back to the New Profession and all the changes that have had a negative effect on many chiropractic practices. This brings me back to the chiropractic gurus. Where'd they go?

It's really simply about supply and demand. Since it requires a completely different and much more comprehensive skill set to thrive today, many of the practice-management coaches have either closed their businesses or have had their businesses greatly reduced because the diminished demand from chiropractors. It takes a systematic approach to thrive today, which will be described to you in detail in the chapters in this very book.

So, we have chiropractors who want nothing more than to deliver a really good service to their patients and expect to receive fair exchange in return but are left holding the bag while new patient numbers are dropping and clinic income is plummeting. This is a prescription for disaster, and it's a reality for MANY, if not, MOST chiropractors today. Know this: You CAN THRIVE in the New Profession!

The New Profession is totally different from the reality of the previous economy. To think that you can simply place some ads in the newspaper and expect the new patients to fly in is akin to expecting a model T Ford to get you from California to Ohio without breaking down. It won't happen. To think it will is delusionary at best. This type of thinking is what is happening in chiropractic. Together, let's change it.

You see, most DCs are practicing what I call 1990s chiropractic. A new patient comes in and gets shuffled off to an "exam room." In the exam room, the patient receives a thorough exam by a well-intentioned doc, and then the patient is released to return the next day for a Report of Findings (ROF).

On day two, the patient comes in and gets shuttled to the ROF room, which is kind of like a shrine to the doc, with all his diplomas and awards gracing the walls. Some ROF rooms may even have really cool mahogany desks and cabinets and shelves filled with yet more accolades and family pictures. This type of ROF room was taught to the profession by the 1980s and 1990s coaches. It's become inefficient in the New Profession.

There is a total lack of efficiency created, as well as a waste of space, by having one or two rooms dedicated to exams and Reports of Findings, ROFs. What's worse is that this concept also creates what I call a **Personality- Dependent Practice**.

The '90s are gone. Exam rooms and ROF rooms should be eliminated. The crazy thing is that most of the DCs I meet today are still practicing with those rooms! Usually, they ask me, "What am I supposed to do with these rooms, then?"

The answer is truly simple: Use them for patient care. I'll show you how shortly, so keep reading!

Then the doc will usually make a statement such as "I already have a couple of adjusting rooms" or "I have open adjusting [which needs to be changed too…more on that later] and don't need any more space."

In the New Profession, the rules of success are very, very different from years past. Your practice must evolve, or it will be adversely affected.

The New Profession demands excellence and efficiency. It's not that people are any smarter; we aren't. But we are more knowledgeable, and that's due to the ease of the flow of information on the Internet. Patients are demanding the very best. Roller tables, e-stim, and ultrasound are not the best…not even close. They are holdovers from the 1970s that many, many chiropractic practices still utilize as if they were really effective. They aren't. They are *very* old technology. Let's group massage in that category, too. Massage belongs in the salon down the street, where it's expected to be delivered. To do massage in a professional practice is to put your practice on par with a barbershop. That being said, using classic massage for promotion can be very beneficial to your practice. Using massage this way can allow you the opportunity to expose more people to your chiropractic services. We will talk about what type of muscle work is getting far better results than classic massage in this book, so please do not go fire your massage therapist!

I go to a barbershop that cuts only males' hair. It's like a man cave, a den of testosterone. TVs are all over the place. You can get a free beer if you want one, and they'll even give you a shave! If I want a massage, I'll go there! It's all part of the New Profession shift in how and where services are delivered. Soon, you'll totally understand this concept.

Before I go any further, I want to say that the New Profession has exacted many pressures on a chiropractic practice. Below is a list of the 10 top angst-inducing pressures now facing chiropractors. Ignore them at your peril. Also know that they do NOT have to be present in your life. Here's the list:

1. New Patient numbers are low.
2. Average Visit Income is low.
3. Personality- Dependent Practices are the prevalent model.
4. Minimal systems are in place.
5. Docs are forced to always work "in" their practices.
6. Audits are accelerating.

7. Exit strategies are not plentiful.
8. Poor insurance coverage abounds.
9. EOBs are wrongfully denied.
10. Chiropractic sees only 7.2% of Americans, at best.

As we delve more deeply into this book, I'll endeavor to give you solid, concrete, tested and proven methods—evolved methods—to accurately address these stress creators. Suffice it to say, chiropractic is changing faster than ever before. Chiropractors must remain current and must continually evolve their practice if they want lasting success. It boils down to this: Evolve your practice so you can truly have a dynamite practice and personal lifestyle, and base your practice on a simple premise, which is to always ask yourself what's best for the patient.

Here's what NOT to do, or pay attention to: ads touting the latest and greatest piece of equipment that will save your practice. Statements such as "Triple your practice in just 60 days" should be totally ignored. Let's always make our greatest concern what's best for the patient.

What I'd like to know is, where is the emphasis is on improving the OUTCOMES of treatment programs in most of the ads in our journals? In other words, how does this gizmo translate into better proven results for my patients? Who gives a darn if you can triple your practice in 60 days while walking around the house in your underwear if your patients' results aren't better? I say this a bit tongue in cheek, but really, let's focus on our patients!

I'm going to let you in on a closely held HealthSource secret: You DON'T need any new shiny piece of equipment to evolve your patient outcomes. To the contrary, what works best today is entirely low tech and inexpensive. Stay with me, and I'll explain in this book. The purveyors of expensive equipment will be outraged, and so be it. Please don't be fooled by their ads and testimonials. It's all marketing and it's about selling equipment while taking your money.

Most of the DCs I speak with for the first time are heavy on equipment and low on patients or clinic income—or they have thriving practices but no ability to unplug from them. Low clinic income is just a symptom. Owning too much equipment is also a symptom.

Truth be told, the demographics of today tell me that chiropractors should be thriving like never before. Did you know that roughly 50% of chiropractic college graduates are out of chiropractic entirely in just five years? 50 percent! This is crazy! It does *NOT* need to be this way, not by a long shot. Evolving chiropractic practices is the key to thriving, and ALL DCs are capable of this evolution, especially because it doesn't involve buying all kinds of equipment.

Meanwhile, the baby boomers, the holders of the largest amount of wealth in America, are hitting age 65 to the tune of 10,000 a day. In case you haven't looked at the demographics and psychographics, baby boomers *do not* want to age. They are getting older, kicking and screaming along the way. They are spending money like no other generation in the history of the world in order to *not* feel and look older. The boomers need chiropractic care and have the means to afford it. If they aren't flooding your practice, they should be!

In case I lost you on a couple of words in the last paragraph, let me define them for you.

> **Psychographics:** market research or statistics classifying population groups according to psychological variables (as attitudes, values, or fears) (Webster's Dictionary)

> **Demographics:** relating to the dynamic balance of a population especially with regard to density and capacity for expansion or decline (Webster's Dictionary)

Baby Boomers should be streaming into chiropractic offices like salmon swimming upstream in fall. The *RIGHT* messages and the *RIGHT* treatment provided to them are absolutely key. Without that recipe, it just won't work.

And let me tell you, trying to attract Boomers with the latest and greatest social media fad is a total waste of time and resources. It just doesn't work. It never will. Success today with the Boomers, generation X, generation Y, the millennials, and pretty much any other group or subgroup is found in a manner distinctly different from those methods used in years past. The old way is dead, never to return. It's Old School. New School is needed in your practice, and you're about to learn what that's all about.

The groundwork has been laid. You've got a good inkling on what this book is going to delve into and explore, which is identifying and laying out the answers to practice success in the New Profession. The rules have changed, and so must chiropractors. Evolution, once circumspect, is now crucial. You can learn this practice evolution and put into place for yourself and your practice. You can thrive in practice while also having a life. Let's go to work!

CHAPTER 2

Please, NO More Government Cheese

"It's not enough that we do our best; sometimes we have to do what's required."

—Sir Winston Churchill

Before delving deeply into giving your practice the Ultimate Practice Adjustment, which partly means to evolve your practice into what it truly takes to survive and thrive in the New Profession, it's probably a good idea for you to understand a bit about my journey in chiropractic. It may lend a bit of credibility to what you are reading. You see, I was no different than most in our great profession, in that I was living exactly how Thoreau described most people, in that we tend to "live quiet lives of desperation." And that pretty much sums up my first year in practice.

My undergraduate trek was quite a bit different than for most DCs. I graduated from Ohio University with a Bachelor's of Business Administration…with a ton of science classes thrown in for good measure. This was done partly at the urging of my late father, Mike Tomshack, who was my greatest role model and mentor.

He was fond of telling me that most docs, while certainly smart, did not even know how to balance their checking accounts, and he subtly suggested some business courses in addition to the standard, highly boring premed curriculum.

I remember sitting in my third organic chemistry class, literally bored unconscious, when I made up my mind that I hated most of my science classes and would change my major to business. I knew I loved business. And besides, at OU, no business classes were held on Fridays. So let's see, that means not two- but three-day weekends every single week! This sounded like a winner to me.

So, for my sophomore year, I switched from premed to business. I also competed for and won a full academic scholarship with the Air Force in their ROTC program in the second half of freshman year. I was putting myself through college because I didn't want to be a drain on my parents, and this seemed to be a great way to do it if I could win one of the few scholarships per university. To win one, you had to do really well on a specialized, extremely long test, kind of similar to the SAT but with some really strange stuff thrown in, like dials and gauges and weird pilot questions. Since I wasn't able to even afford the darn study guide, the test was a huge surprise for me.

I distinctly remember taking that test. I woke up early Saturday to write the exam only to discover I had the flu. My head was pounding. I had a fever. The room was spinning and I was nauseated. I felt doomed. I trudged off to take the exam anyway.

When I finished the 15-minute walk to the building, I was no better off. I sat down and did the best I could do. Somewhere deep inside me, the energy was summoned and I was able to concentrate fairly well. By the time I finished, five hours later, I walked back to the dorm and collapsed. Somehow, it all worked out and I won the full-tuition scholarship, free books, and a monthly stipend award. I took the deal. What the heck, it was only a seven-year commitment post graduation!

To completely make ends meet, I became an RA (resident assistant) sophomore year and continued this job all the way through college. I ended up actually making money as an undergrad and even bought a new car, a Honda CRX—red, of course.

What I haven't yet mentioned is that my plan was to become an orthopedic surgeon, not a chiropractor. Plans change. In the summer between my freshman and sophomore years, I was working out with my close friend Ty Hildum. We were supposed to do bench presses and go for an all-out max rep, doing stupid things like 19-year-olds do naturally. Well, Ty didn't show up and I decided to do a one-rep max anyway…without a spotter. Stupid idea.

I hoisted up the weight and slowly dropped it to my chest. There it sat. I couldn't move it. Well, somehow, I got it off my chest and back up on the bar, and while doing that, I felt a searing pain in my neck and upper back. It hurt bad, real bad. I immediately went home.

I couldn't move, and the pain just got worse during the rest of the day. The next morning, it was much worse. My dad had to help me get my head off the pillow. I did everything you're supposed to con-ventionally do to get better. The days ticked off, and I was no better. The guy I was working for in my summer job told me to go to his chiropractor. I didn't even know what a chiropractor was, but I was desperate. I went.

The doc did just what good chiros all know how to do. I got better, quickly. From then on, I knew I was to be a chiropractor. It would just take a circuitous route to get there.

So now it was a couple weeks before graduation and I knew that I was to become a pilot for seven years in the Air Force and then go back to chiro school. This was 1987, and the government started drastically reducing pilot levels. Surprise! There were no pilot slots available unless you were an engineer. I was a business major with a ton of science, so even though I graduated #1 in my ROTC class, which is supposed to darn near guarantee great things in your military career, I was shut out.

My commander told me I could become a navigator instead of a pilot. What that amounts to is that you study charts and dials and gauges and don't get to fly the damn plane. I think not! Flying backseat would run contrary to my highly Type-A personality. I asked him what other options I had. He told me that for the first time in 20–30 years, if I could find a position in the Air Guard, I wouldn't have to go active duty at all. I could be a weekend warrior instead! He gave me a list of phone numbers.

I grabbed the list with sweaty hands. I clearly remember sprinting all the way to the other side of the campus to my dorm so I could start dialing for freedom, knowing full well that tons of other college ROTC seniors would be doing the same thing that day. I got lucky—very, very lucky—and secured an interview with a Guard base right in Ohio, about 90 minutes from home. It was for a supply officer position. I didn't know what that was and didn't care. I just knew it meant that I wouldn't have to be a navigator for seven long, boring, backseat years staring at dials.

I got the job! At this time, I knew I didn't have enough money to go to chiropractic school, so I started interviewing for jobs. I got one with a company that had a really good training program, so I took it. That ate up the entire summer, with the occasional weekend at the Air Guard base once a month. I graduated at the top of the training class and won the best region, the upper west coast…which was the last place on earth I wanted to be because that would mean I would now be a six-hour plane flight from the love of my life, Lisa Lorenzo.

I declined the position, much to the chagrin of my boss, who just about had an aneurysm right there in his office. I quickly called some business colleges to see about starting an MBA program, but since I had no money, I'd need to win a position as a teaching assistant.

Good fortune prevailed, and I earned just such a position at Toledo University. Classes started about two weeks later. I thought this would be perfect. I could learn more about business, which I love, then head to chiropractic school. I was in for a rude awakening.

I had hoped to accelerate my business acumen by getting an MBA. I quickly learned that not only was the college using the SAME textbooks as I'd used in undergrad, but the classes were as boring as organic chemistry! Same books as undergrad, just a ton more homework and projects. And the professors also managed to make the classes hyper-insanely boring. To top it off, my teaching assistant job consisted of boring research and essentially making copies for a professor who had the personality of a snail. Crazy! I finished the first term and decided I'd had enough of this madness.

I still needed to earn some money to get to chiropractic college, so I took a job as a food broker for a few years, learning more about real-world, relevant business while stockpiling cash. All the while, I took some night classes at Cleveland State to finish up all the science requirements I hadn't gotten in business school. I applied and was accepted to Palmer University.

Well, those were 10 more fun-filled trimesters! I was also the school peer counselor, which cut my tuition in half. Lisa and I got married two weeks prior to matriculation, which I wouldn't recommend for a great start to a marriage. I was holed up studying, leaving her to watch our tiny black-and-white 12" TV in the freezing living room of our rickety, leaky-roofed, 1964 mobile home with the ceiling caving in.

Fortunately, Lisa stayed with me, which seemed a bit dicey the first year, especially our first Christmas holiday. She also enrolled in the CT program out of boredom and absolutely excelled! Then she got pregnant, to boot. She delivered Shannon 24 hours before she graduated and, like the trooper she was and is, she walked across the stage a mere one day after delivery! Shannon was born smack in the middle of seventh-trimester finals week.

Because I finished all my clinical "numbers" just two weeks in to my ninth trimester, I had to turn over all my patients to other students having trouble. I always felt that was socialism. Worse, I now had nothing to do, so I found a preceptorship for 10th trimester and found a building, an old converted home, back in our hometown and bought it. A banker, Mr. Ed Klenz, then gave me a loan for $40,000 so we could remodel it. He gave me that loan while I was still a student! I credit Mr. Klenz with significantly helping me launch my career, and I am eternally indebted to his kindness.

Oh, I almost forgot, in ninth trimester, we had some kind of finance class at Palmer. I went in to talk to the professor about testing out because I had studied business at the graduate level. He was not impressed. He grudgingly gave me the okay to right a paper to test out. I passed. He then told me he highly recommended that I not skip his class or I wouldn't be successful. I wonder where this guy is today?

So Lisa and I, me at age 29 and Lisa at 28, launched our first practice on March 7, 1994. Times were slow. Business was slower. I had no money and, not many patients, and even though I had a business degree, I didn't know what to do with it, how to apply it. We were forced to go on welfare, and food stamps. And every Tuesday morning, the government cheese truck would drop off about 20 pounds of cheese and milk. You can only eat so much cheese before things begin to bind up way down low in your colon. Finally, I was trading my siblings' cheese for other items or just plain giving the cheese away, just trying to stay regular.

I was a failure that first year. I knew I needed help. I hired a guru, Dr. Bob Sottile. He was helpful. He helped me see that the possibilities were far greater than my present reality. More than anything else, that was his greatest contribution. The practice grew. I hired another guru, Dr. Fred Schofield. Dr. Fred is the world's best motivator. He helped me expand my horizons. I started reading all types of books: books on motivation, books on self-development, and books on business. I started studying other industries, looking for business principles I could apply to my practice. This was when we really exploded! The practice was now HUGE.

I retired from active practice in 2002 so the clinic could grow even more. I hired many associate doctors. In 2004, Lisa and I opened another clinic and quickly built it into a million-dollar clinic. In one stretch, I went eight months without even going to the clinic. Yes, that's possible when the clinic is run correctly. Then we opened two more clinics, both very large. Then, in one crystal-clear moment, I realized that we had built a model, probably the first such model in chiropractic, that wasn't built on a doctor's personality. It was replicable. We should start a chiropractic franchise.

We were off and running.

In April 2006, we sold our first franchise. Dr. Chad quickly, following exactly what we told him to do (most of the time, anyway), built a huge practice in record time from the shell of a practice he had built thus far. We've now evolved HealthSource into the largest chiropractic family in the world.

During this evolutionary process, which continues constantly, we've chosen complete autonomy. We're a bit like outsiders and choose to remain so. Unless you remove yourself from the repetitive thinking processes, evolution is really not possible. Our model is entirely different from what was taught in years past. Coaches today are still teaching people to build personality-dependent practices. We don't. Others teach basic processes. We teach business systems to run everything. Meanwhile, equipment salesmen teach docs to buy overpriced miracle equipment when it comes to patient care. We teach that it's all about the relentless pursuit of exceptional care for the right reasons, not to goose the clinic numbers. We tell the truth as we see it.

Our quest for the relentless pursuit of exceptional care demands that we remain "new school." What worked in the '90s and up to 2012 no longer works. It now fails miserably. We now live in a New Profession with a completely new set of rules, rendering old-school advice not only obsolete but also damaging in terms of compliance in many cases. It must be about doing what is right for the patient, first and foremost. If that isn't the cornerstone upon which a practice is built, the practice will not continue to succeed.

CHAPTER 3

Here's What Won't Work

"Success is a lousy teacher. It seduces smart people into thinking they can't lose."

—Bill Gates

The depressing news is that many practices across America are shrinking or, at best, stagnant while the cost to run a practice continues to escalate. Medico-legal risk is skyrocketing faster than an intercontinental ballistic missile threat from North Korea. Third-party audits are decimating even the most stable practices at a record pace. In short, it's much harder to be successful today in chiropractic than ever before. But this does NOT have to be your reality!

All that being said, today, it is SIMPLE to run a great practice…simple, but not easy. The days of burying your head in the sand, trudging ahead blindly, all the while still using old- school Travel Cards and tossing patients on Roller Tables while they're hooked up to e-stim, are just about dead… thank God!

I mean, really, since when do roller tables and e-stim answer the fundamental question that all doctors should be asking themselves when designing treatment programs for their patients, which is "What's best for the patient?"

In this chapter, I'm blatantly going to sacrifice MANY sacred cows in chiropractic. It'll likely irritate you to no end; maybe even totally piss you off. My job in writing this book is not to "win friends and influence people"; it's to tell the truth as I see it. And that truth has been gleaned while running the largest family in chiropractic, a family built on high ethics and integrity, a family built solely on answering the question "What's best for the patient?" Note that the question is NOT "What's easiest for the doctor" or "How can I make more money the fastest, responsibilities and fiduciary interest to the patient be damned!"

It's time to grab the dagger and Ginsu knife and go to work slaying those activities that do NOT work in the New Profession. (We're going about our slaughter in no particular order.) While reading the remainder of this chapter, try not to slam the book down, cursing loudly and kicking the unsuspecting family dog. I will go into clinically and ethically correct solutions...just not in this chapter! So please, grab a cup of organic green tea, and let's attack this chapter. You just may wish to have a highlighter in hand as well. Go ahead and grab one now, then get back here and strap in tightly.

Here's What Won't Work To Build Your Practice in The New Profession.

1. Social Media
    Social media can bring in some new patients, just not a lot of them. Social media is the ultimate fool's gold, much like a lot of the Internet marketing being done. Here's the dirty little secret that the purveyors of social media don't want you to know: Social media was NOT created to drive business. It was created to facilitate cyber

friendship in today's world of busyness. It's a method of totally detaching from the real world for multiple segments during your day.

As a result, people are logging in to escape the real world, not to do business with others. It's totally counterintuitive to its designed function. All you have to do is follow the older teenagers to see the trends. Every few years, they migrate from one social medial to the next—i.e., from MySpace to Facebook, then blogging, then YouTube, then Twitter and Pinterest. It's nonstop, and newcomers will continue to pop up and create yet more distraction for you and your team. Avoid these time-wasters. Avoid the people telling you that you must use them to figure out this "new" way to promote your practice.

The critical thing to remember is that these sites are designed to escape reality, not to create business for your clinic. People seem to live on these sites for an escape, not to do business.

That does not mean that you need not have a presence in social media or on the Internet in general. I think you should—but it should be a presence, not an obsession. Much like my first mentor in chiropractic, the late, great Dr. Russell Earhardt, told me years ago when I helped him with his seminars on radiology while a student at Palmer, "Show me a good pool player, and I'll show you a wasted life!" The same can be said for spending any more than about three to five minutes a day on social media, blogging included.

It's been sad to watch the unscrupulous hawkers of social media crank up their ads in our trade journals. It reminds me of the decompression practice debacle, and it should be avoided.

2. SEO: Search-Engine Optimization
    Here's another member of the Fool's Gold Society. You can go totally nuts trying to optimize your search-engine ranking. I'm not telling you that you shouldn't throw a little money at this activity, but it should be *VERY* little. The days of tricking the search engine to rank your practice higher are *GONE*. Good content is king.

    As long as a patient or prospective patient can find you on the Web, you'll be fine. There is no need to ensure that you're always the #1 or #2- ranked chiro when someone searches in your area. Being on the first page of search results is absolutely fine. Don't let any whiz- bang salesman try to convince you otherwise. Just get on the first page and have the link drive to your web page.

    "You mean I need to have a Web page?" Yep. It need not be some super-elaborate series of links, videos, and landing pages. It needs to explain why your practice is the right place to be for the very best in treatment, period. Videos are essential. The page should instill confidence in the prospective patients. Don't oversell. Tell the truth. If your practice is not the best around, you're already behind the eight ball and it's your competitor's shot. Get busy. Answers to this most fundamental evolution are forthcoming in a later chapter. Don't skip ahead. Focus. Concentrate!

3. Yellow Pages
    Wow, do I remember the days of the Yellow Page advertising reps coming into my office, staring me down, and using every high-pressure sales tactic they learned in their boot-camp training program to bully me into buying ever bigger and bigger ads for the four clinics I owned. These guys give used car salesmen a good name.

    But I was always about 10 steps ahead of them. I knew when they would be coming. I had already analyzed all the relevant phone books and determined which ones to have a larger presence in, and I had analyzed the competitors' ads.

Then I analyzed the data regarding my Yellow Page ads of that year and calculated the Return On Investment (ROI), and the answer became obvious on what size ad I should run, if any at all. Then, since I had studied copywriting at the foot of the master, Dan Kennedy, I wrote my Yellow Page ad(s) and had them sent to my graphic designer to finish them up. NEVER let the yellow pages design your ad. They're horrible. They're salespeople, not copywriters.

All that was left to do was step into the octagon with the sales rep and slug out the price. They get bonuses on pushing you to larger ads every year. If you haven't done the preparatory work described a moment ago, you might fall for their chicanery. Don't let that happen.

In short, you want your ROI to be a minimum of 3-to-1, which means that for every dollar you spend, you collect three. Nothing less than 3:1 is acceptable.

Determining ad size is not difficult. If your ad is producing a greater than 3:1 ROI and your competitor has a great ad that is bigger than yours, it's time to move up. First, determine if a really good ad designed by a good copywriter can achieve a greater than 3:1 ROI. If no, consider dropping that phone book altogether. If yes, if your competitor has a good, larger ad, move up to a bigger size.

My goal was to always dominate the good books. But remember this very key point: Yellow Pages will *NOT* save or build your practice. They are merely another fishing pole in the water to drive some business into your clinic. Having said that, I'll point out that most yellow pages are going the way of the brontosaurus: extinct. You MUST do your research, carefully calculate ROI, and determine which books, if any, you should employ.

As I fly across the country visiting our HealthSource clinics, the second thing I do when I get to the hotel is scour the yellow pages. The trend is clear: Ad sizes are down and the quality of the ads is poor. A good ad can still produce new patients if it's the right ad in the right book.

4.   Low Fee and High Volume
This albatross is an energy killer and shoulder destroyer. It's a mantra from very old-school coaches! Truth be told, many people are still preaching this dead horse today.

High volume and low fee is fine if you want to provide outdated service and eventually have a massive cardiac arrest while adjusting a patient when you should have retired 20 years ago but couldn't. This concept is based on what used to be termed "rack 'em and crack 'em." Never is any regard given to the question "What's best for the patient?" Worse, much worse, is that many of these outdated offices put every single patient on the same treatment program...the same one! This is one hugely ethically challenged way to practice. (More on this later.) I get irritated just thinking about this concept. It's universally one of the largest reasons that chiropractic sees only about seven percent of the American population. It's destructive at best, criminal at worst.

Back in my first year of practice, when I was clueless, the love of my life, Lisa, worked with me all day and then immediately after dinner drove a couple of miles to the highly successful dentist in town. She did that so she could clean the dental office for $50 a night. I was such a colossal failure that we desperately needed that $50.

The dentist obviously felt sorry for us and invited us over for dinner. Once there, he sat me down and explained the premise of always asking yourself what's best for the patient. It was a game changer for me. It taught me to focus on the patient, not on me or the practice. It taught me to design a care program that would be best for the patient, without regard for any other factor, a care plan based on what is proven TODAY to be the most beneficial for my patient. I soon discovered something fundamentally true with every single chiropractor:

If you are practicing today the way you were when you graduated, you are already obsolete. Period.

It doesn't matter if you graduated last week. It takes time for colleges to get updated textbooks and to incorporate them into clinical work—lots of time. The very best "stuff" is being discovered daily; it wasn't discovered 25 years ago. If you are to stay relevant and deliver outstanding care, you MUST stay current.

To sum this one up: Fair exchange must occur with each and every patient encounter. Giving away your service is not fair exchange, and neither is overcharging for useless therapy or the newest shiny gizmo that the patient does not need, especially when ways to get far better results exist.

5. The Cash Practice
Seriously? This one grinds me as much as high volume and low fee. What is there about the cash-practice model that answers the question "What's best for the patient?" This is a doctor-centric model that cares about one thing: the doctor.

I don't know about you, but if I had a health challenge that isn't responding to chiropractic care, I'd be a bit steamed if my doctor would not accept my health insurance, wouldn't you? Now, fortunately, I can afford to pay cash, but many cannot. Let me be perfectly clear about where I think we are headed in America: Chiropractic will increasingly become more and more based on patients paying cash for their care as insurance, personal injury, and work comp goes the way of the saber-toothed tiger.

But that's the future, not now. HealthSource teaches that your practice should reflect the demographics of your community. This means that if roughly 60% of your community has insurance coverage, your practice should be about 60% insurance based. Make sense?

Any of these model variations are therefore unhealthy and usually based on one of two questions: "What's best for the doctor" or "How can I generate the most reimbursement humanely possible by becoming a PI mill or Work Comp doc?" If any of these models describe you, please give this topic some good concentration. Let's focus on ethical care for the right reasons, using the best care currently available to ensure that our patients get the highest level of healing.

6. Functional Medicine
    Let's sum up this model with the statement "Here come your state board and patient lawsuits, and up goes your stress levels right into the stratosphere." Personally, I've seen offices attempt this model and fail miserably. Frankly, the docs I'm talking about were running million-dollar practices. Every single time the docs ran down this road, *every single time*, it destroyed their practice.

    Did I mention that every single practice was hurt?

Most of the functional-medicine programs out there attempt to teach you how to work with patients who have endocrine or diabetic conditions. This is a high-risk population. Usually, the patient is put on a restrictive diet. Truth be told, I'm gluten free and dairy free and have been for years. I've totally eliminated my allergies as a very cool side effect. But most patients either cannot or will not stick to the diet. Then they are usually put through cleanses followed by extremely expensive supplementation designed to "balance the organs and the body."

As this fad generated steam, you could see the ads appear in our trade journals: "Generate a million dollars in seven months!" In typical fashion, many docs took the bait hook, line, and sinker. Major problems soon followed.

Why? Most DC's do not have the additional post doctoral classes to truly understand real functional wellness, let alone know what to do when their patient's diabetic markers start going the wrong way. The most devastating and damaging thing that occurs as a direct result of chasing functional- medicine money is that it simply takes your eye off your core competency, which is chiropractic. What ensues in the office of almost every doc who uses functional medicine is serious problems: Their primary chiropractic practice suffers as they take their eye off it, and ultimately, their functional- medicine foray is abandoned. I'm not saying it does not help compliant patients, because that would be wrong. I've seen compliant patients get tremendous results. Unfortunately, I've seen a ton of practices hurt, too.

7.   Personal Injury
      To many unsuspecting chiropractors, converting their practice to a personal- injury model may seem at first blush a smart and prudent way to structure their practice. Truth be told, however, the 1990s are over.

In the 1980s, 1990s and into the 21st century, personal-injury practices thrived in certain states or areas of the country. Essentially, this is no longer the truth. In most states, laws and regulations have passed that have converted the once highly lucrative personal-injury chiropractic practice model into a model that no longer functions anywhere near the level at which it used to function.

All this being said, this is a very good thing to occur. The personal-injury model of practice has been one of the most damaging types of practice in chiropractic's history. Doctors in search of the easy dollar were drawn to this model in droves. As a result, many unnecessary, and or, unethical paradigms evolved.

State-by-state, as each jurisdiction began to place limits on personal- injury reimbursement (and, at the very least, make the doctor accountable for his or her actions), the personal-injury model began to thankfully disappear. There are, as of today, still a few holdout pockets in the country, but those are rapidly disappearing.

Now, if, in the course of a day, a new patient walks into the clinic and is a personal-injury patient, I highly encourage you to give that patient the absolute best level of care with respect and integrity and get him or her better. That's how chiropractic shines, and that's how you shine. To chase the personal-injury dollar without regard for the patient is just plain wrong.

About 15 years ago when the state in which I used to practice changed the personal-injury laws, it was with great relief that I saw the personal-injury mills shut down. Fortunately, there's really no place left for these types of practices today.

8. Neuropathy
    As I'm writing this book, this is one of the trendiest niches that the magic bullet-seeking chiropractors are

attracted to. In all seriousness, this is nothing more than a spinal-decompression debacle of 2005 repeated all over again with a different color lipstick on the same pig. Chasing conditions WILL divert your attention from your core competence: chiropractic.

With these neuropathy-styled practices, the chiropractors typically place ads in newspapers, essentially promoting themselves as some sort of specialist in treating neuropathy conditions. I find this perplexing, mostly because these chiropractors purport to have some new magic cold laser that miraculously and mysteriously cures patients of their neuropathy without regard to the cause. In my mind, this is akin to simply choking down some pain pills when you've got a burning pain in your shoulder: The pain is alleviated as you take the pills, but the cause of the pain is never treated and therefore continues to get worse over time. I am *not* saying that symptomatic relief is not important, because it is, but let's make sure we're treating the cause of the pain too.

If we take a look at the chiropractic profession since 1895, we see that we have been, in many cases, treating the cause of various neuropathies all along. There is nothing new here, other than the claim that some new gizmo is actually going to treat the cause of the problem as opposed to simply treating the symptoms. Oh, and the gizmo is very expensive. Then you must also have the "magic ads" guaranteed to quadruple your practice while you sit at home in your underwear.

9. Weight Loss
    This one will get you so far off track that you may never recover. I've got a great deal of firsthand experience with state-of-the-art weight-loss programs that are practice proven, probably more so than just about any other chiropractor on the planet. We've learned some lessons— some hard lessons.

If you're a chiropractor reading this, someday, simply take a walk out in the reception room and take a good, hard look at your patients. Perhaps do it tomorrow. Are they all in great shape? Is everyone at an ideal weight and body composition? Or are you confronted with a great preponderance of people who really need to lose weight to achieve a healthier lifestyle? Yep, that's what I thought, most of them have some serious pounds to lose.

Next you have to ask yourself how to best help your patients lose weight. Do you send them to the doc down the street who's never even had a single classroom hour in nutrition? How about sending them to one of the weight-loss mills where they can buy some prepackaged and highly synthetic, sugar-laden garbage food? Oh wait, I know, how about we put them on a 500-calorie-a-day diet and give them some magic drops and watch the pounds melt off?

I am firmly committed to the belief that there are a number of chiropractors out there who can truly and effectively and efficiently help patients lose weight. These doctors are in the minority in our profession, however.

Just as an aside, it's really not that difficult to lose weight. I've co-written another book on weight loss (*Freedom from Fat*), and the literature continues to provide reams of information on the very best and most effective ways to lose weight. It is not magic. It is not a mystery. It's science. And it's actually simple. It's not easy, but it's simple.

So, for the other 98% of the chiropractic professionals out there, attempting to run a weight-loss business within your clinic is tantamount to jumping off a bridge without a bungee cord attached.

The primary reason why attempting to run a weight-loss business within your practice is so destructive is much the same as trying to run many other types of niche businesses within your practice: It pulls you from your core competency, which is chiropractic care for your patients. That being said, if I were still in practice today, I would most certainly be helping my patients lose weight in a healthy, effective, and non-synthetic fashion for a lifetime of wellness. It's not hard.

10. Cold Laser

Attempting to base your practice on cold-laser therapy is not good. This is also a very confusing topic to most chiropractors. All you've got to do is open our trade journals to see a plethora of advertisements expounding on why one type of laser is better than the other. The class IV laser manufacturers are blasting the class II lasers, and so on. It gets crazy. How is a chiropractor supposed to understand what is and is not most effective for patients?

The one thing that must be discussed when talking about cold-laser therapy is that it is highly palliative in nature. We must never forget that as chiropractors, our mission and primary focus is to always address the cause of whatever is interfering with the wellness and lifestyle of the patient in front of us. To merely treat the symptom is to ignore the cause. To ignore the cause is to guarantee that the symptom returns. Treat the cause.

In HealthSource, many of our practices utilize cold lasers. We don't necessarily promote any one manufacturer, as many of them have some benefits. Many of them are also fairly useless. What we do counsel our HealthSource family on is addressing the cause of symptoms. If you want to use cold-laser therapy to help alleviate symptoms in the short term, go for it, but above all else, fix the cause of the problem.

Other than treating symptoms while ignoring causes, the biggest detriment of trying to run a cold laser-based practice is that you begin to chase very specific conditions or diagnoses. This results in the same thing as some of the other niches that I've previously discussed: It will take your focus off your core business, which is chiropractic care. Doctors tend to lose their focus with it, and their practices begin to drop.

11. Nutrition
We could write chapters on this particular topic alone, so I'll attempt to keep this as brief as humanly possible. Let me start with a simple question: who in their right mind would jam known, cancer-causing synthetic vitamins into their bodies? Chiropractors should know better. Probably the most knowledgeable individual on the planet with regard to this topic is Dr. James Chestnut from Innate Choice. For a primer, I would highly encourage you to go to his website and begin to read the mountains of information via the links that he has posted there.

Running a practice that is basically 50% or above nutrition-based, meaning 50% or more of the income derived in your clinic is strictly from the sale of nutritional products and the counseling on thereof, is in almost every case barely a break-even endeavor. By and large, the great preponderance of "nutrition practices" barely get by and pay their bills. Many sources exist from which people can purchase nutrition. Nutrition stores are all over the place. Why would you willingly convert a chiropractic practice into a nutrition store?

This doesn't even begin to address the fact that synthetic vitamins can cause cancer. It's proven. It's not open for discussion. Most vitamins out there, even those that make wild claims that they are 100% natural, are, in fact, synthetic. Just because the vitamin was cultured in a yeast environment does not mean it is natural, although the manufacturers are allowed to claim this. The vitamin is in fact chemically synthetic. Synthetic vitamins can cause cancer. I do not put them in my body, nor do I put them in my family's bodies.

To simplify nutrition, it's easiest to simply analyze what our patients' most basic needs are, keeping in mind that slamming down some synthetic vitamins is not in their best interests. Yes, you can certainly boost the bottom line of your clinic by recommending all sorts of synthetic vitamins, but can you ethically balance that in your mind and heart?

Dr. Chestnut has this topic totally nailed. We've incorporated, after much due diligence, his recommendations regarding offering HealthSource patients the essential supplements necessary for a healthy lifestyle and wellness environment. These include

A.   Essential omega-3 fish oil supplementation,
B.   Essential vitamin D3 supplementation, and
C.   Essential probiotic supplementation.

When a truly 100% natural and organic multivitamin becomes available, that would definitely be added to the list. In the meantime, what we advise our patients to do at home in lieu of a 100% natural multivitamin is to invest in a machine such as a Vita-Mix and at the very least use it to concoct an absolutely incredible breakfast. Here's what I have for breakfast: a glass of filtered water; organic and gluten-free oatmeal; rice- or egg-based protein; and tons of organic spinach, broccoli, kale, and other green leafy vegetables. Throw in ½ cup of organic coconut milk and blend this thing for about a minute. The machine will pulverize all the ingredients into a delectable, nutrient-dense breakfast that simply can't be beat. If you want to increase your energy level, try this on for size every morning. I often have one for lunch. In fact just today, I filmed a video on making one of these incredible drinks. You can check it out on the Health-Source Chiropractic YouTube channel.

12. An Adjusting-Only Practice model

Wow, and I thought that as new discoveries were made to help our patients get better with a much deeper level of healing to help maximize recovery and prevent recurrences of their presenting problems, it would seem natural to constantly upgrade and evolve our level of care for patients. Strangely enough, this isn't the case with a percentage of chiropractors.

A practice model whereby the doctor only performs chiropractic adjustments certainly can provide help to patients. But why not treat patients as you would want to be treated if you had a problem? An adjustment-only model is straight out of about 1910. Many of the docs who practice in this fashion do so because they claim that the developer of chiropractic, Dr. B. J. Palmer, practiced that way. Point of fact: This is inaccurate.

While performing this very same research myself more than 20 years ago, I came across pictures of Dr. B. J. Palmer's "rehab" facility at the Palmer school of chiropractic. What set his rehab department apart from a typical rehab department was that his was based on "functional" rehabilitation. That term had not yet been coined during his lifetime, but careful examination of the equipment that was utilized in his facility clearly shows that it was based on multi-joint and compound movements affecting most of the body. This was the earliest form of functional rehabilitation that I've been able to find. And the cool thing is that it is greatly evolved today.

Chiropractors who practice an adjustment-only model clearly seem to have forgotten or choose to ignore the fact that muscular imbalances and asymmetries often lead to the presenting problems that they see manifested in their patients. To correct misalignments or subluxations only yields short-term changes because the imbalances and asymmetries are never addressed. For this reason, the problems recur over and over again, so an adjustment-only model, in my mind, provides only about one third of the solution for patients. Nutrition and the muscular system are totally neglected, allowing the patient to never achieve true wellness.

Oh, and by the way, I contend that if a chiropractor is practicing the way he or she did when they graduated, even if graduation was just a year ago, the chiropractor is practicing in an obsolete fashion. Amazing discoveries are being made virtually every day in our field, and to ignore them is to put blinders on. Unfortunately, this is one of the largest problems affecting chiropractic today. I believe that most of this has occurred because chiropractors by and large tend to be lone rangers all alone on their own islands, not associating with anybody else and therefore limiting their interactions with the evolutionary changes that are available. This is a HUGE mistake, and patients suffer as a result.

HealthSource has fixed this problem by becoming the largest family in chiropractic in the world with regular local, regional, and national meetings at which we present all the newest findings so we can continuously engage in the relentless pursuit of exceptional care and offer that exceptional care to our patients whenever it's deemed necessary. These weekly, monthly, quarterly, and yearly gatherings also serve to bring our chiropractors together for a fresh exchange of ideas and camaraderie, which has been sorely lacking in our great profession.

13. Passive Therapy (aka the Great Roller Table and E-Stim Proliferation)

Passive therapy was high tech until about 1970. To be very blunt, roller tables are very old school. They mostly provide very little, though, yes, they feel good.

Why is it, then, that well over 50% of chiropractic practices seem to have these outdated pterodactyls in their offices? Some docs are billing insurance companies for them and coding it as traction. This is illegal. Roller tables, or intersegmental traction, is not, by definition, classical traction, nor is it legal to be billed to insurance companies or patients as such. That is fraud.

Electrical stimulation and ultrasound are different than roller tables in that they do have some therapeutic benefit, most often in the extreme short term. Frankly, I'm of the opinion that patients should be transitioned off of either modality as quickly as humanly possible, usually in a matter of a few days of care. There are many far more effective ways to help your patients in addition to providing outstanding chiropractic technique.

Case in point, the excessive and extensive use of passive care within the chiropractic arena is one of the primary reasons so many chiropractic clinics are getting audited by third-party payers these days. (There are a host of other reasons for these audits that we'll get into in a later chapter.)

Suffice it to say, passive therapy of all types is extremely old school and is not even in the same universe of effectiveness as active forms of care. Research proves this over and over again. What makes this even more challenging is that active care is evolving constantly. What is the best today will not be the best tomorrow, and we as chiropractors must constantly strive to stay abreast of what works the very, very best now, *today!* At HealthSource, we show our doctors all the newest advances with the most efficacious therapeutic benefit each and every year because so much changes in just 12 months. Don't your patients deserve the best?

14. Exercise: Old School vs. New School
   A modest number of chiropractic clinics are now finally offering soft-tissue work, notably therapeutic exercise, as a means to facilitate a much better level of healing in their patients. The problem is that most chiropractors are doing or performing old-school exercise. Changes are being made in exercise constantly, at breakneck speed.

   Typically, when I come into contact with our chiropractors who are using exercise, they are usually using McKenzie or Williams protocols. These were high-tech a very long time ago. They don't compare in results with functional movement-based exercises. Talk about an evolution! Functional exercise is just plain light years ahead. The results are amazing, simply amazing.

   The challenge occurs with a chiropractor that is trying very hard to take care of her patients while at the same time staying abreast of all the newest scientific advances in patient care. It's just about impossible. There aren't enough hours in the day to do both.

   Just a few short weeks prior to writing this chapter, I was researching some of the newest and most effective ways possible via functional exercise to work with patients who are having chronic shoulder issues. What I found was simply mind blowing. I used the techniques on my own bilateral chronic shoulder issues. Prior to using them, I had been using what most chiropractors and physical therapists would consider to be absolute state-of-the-art exercises. I was wrong. The newest exercises and stretches are worlds ahead of what we thought was high tech just last year. I was ecstatic to learn of these advances!

So as a result, we'll be certifying all of the hundreds of HealthSource offices across the country in these brand-new techniques very soon. Who benefits? The patients benefit, because that's what matters. The relentless pursuit of exceptional care is what separates the mediocre from the great.

15. Massage

Please don't get me started on this one. Where do most people go to receive a massage? Guess what, it's not a chiropractor's office. It's at a salon or barbershop or dedicated massage office. This has been the recent transition.

Most of the time massage is provided in a chiropractic setting, it is massage of the classical nature, meaning that it is what I call foo-foo massage. And that simply means that it's therapeutically ineffective in achieving long-term substantive changes in a patient. Yes, the patients may feel relieved for a short period of time, but once they're back in their normal environments, nothing is changed. People are also now conditioned that massage is associated with barbershops.

This is not to say that working with a patient's soft tissue is not appropriate at times, because it most certainly can be appropriate. And when I'm talking about appropriate soft-tissue work, I'm talking about functional-based deep-tissue work. In other words, if your patient is smiling when receiving our brand of deep-tissue massage, the massage is not being done correctly.

If you want to truly strip down adhesions within the muscular tissue and reactivate certain muscles, foo-foo massage just won't get it done. And functional-based deep-tissue work is also evolving. At one time, many chiropractors used all sorts of expensive metal devices to apply pressure to the soft tissue to facilitate healing. That was high tech a long time ago. It's not necessary today—not if you're using the most evolved techniques. As a matter of fact, it's very inexpensive to provide the most effective means of functional-based deep-tissue work, exercise, or stretching utilizing the most evolved protocols.

Classic massage can be used in a chiropractic setting for promotional reasons, such as exposing more people to chiropractic care through a carefully designed marketing program designed to bring people in for a classic massage and then, if the patient is a good candidate, continue with an offering for a chiropractic exam at a future date.

16. Marketing
   Okay, I'm going to be really brief on this one. The most effective marketing on the planet will not fix substandard care or service. For years, chiropractors have been searching for the magic-bullet marketing technique that will turbo-charge their practices, but the truth is, they should've been evolving their care instead. It is a much better investment.

   This isn't to say that marketing is unnecessary. I believe it most certainly is necessary in <u>all</u> cases, especially if your practice is a personality-dependent practice, which most are. But chasing the next new marketing gimmick is not going to save a chiropractic practice. It may provide a short-term blip in new patients and income, but that increase is short-lived.

   All marketing becomes stale. Let me say this again: All marketing becomes stale. All marketing pieces as well as all marketing genres wear out. First fix your product. Then worry about the marketing.

17. Hiring Associates

Here's another potential major headache. When chiropractors hire associate doctors to come into the practice, they do so under the guise of growing their practices. This couldn't be further from the truth. In fact, hiring new associates often harms rather than helps your practice. It's the sad truth that the typical chiropractor is ill equipped to train and does not know how to effectively train an associate so to fulfill the role for which the associate was brought into the practice in the first place.

So here's how a typical training session goes when the chiropractor hires an associate. The owner-doc says, "I'm gonna have you follow me around for a few weeks, and then I'll let you start seeing some of my patients. We'll start with the Medicaid patients, then we'll see how it goes." It usually doesn't even make it to the Medicaid-patient stage. This training program is highly deficient, yet it's the norm. I did this with my first (and second) associate, too!

If you want your associate to actually help grow your practice, they must be trained correctly. In fact, the training never stops…ever. I teach that you must hold a pre-scripted, minimum three-hour training program each and every week while the associate is on your team. If you expect them to achieve greatness, and they can, they must be led correctly. The old adage is that there are no bad students, only bad teachers. I concur. Sometimes, however, you may not be the correct teacher to "reach" a doctor to ensure great learning takes place. We must recognize when this is a reality and give some other doc a try.

In HealthSource, we have 26 different modules that we rotate twice each year in order to conduct highly effective training programs, not just for the associate doctor but also for the entire team, as well as the chiropractor that owns the clinic. The greatest sports figures of our time all have mentors. They do this because it works and it's necessary. I have mentors as well. To assume that you do not need a mentor or someone to simply hold you accountable for you to achieve practice greatness is delusionary. Get a mentor! Be the mentor for your team and your family.

I don't want to sound too flippant about getting a mentor, because I, like many others, have made some pretty poor choices when trying to find the correct mentor. In our profession, virtually every coach out there will teach you how to build a personality- dependent practice. So if you're successful at this, you've still built a jail from which you can't escape. You must find a mentor that teaches you how to build a practice that is no longer dependent upon your personality. That's building a business and not a job.

18. The Guru
    Earlier, I sort of touched on hiring a guru to help you achieve success. I like success-based, non-personality-dependent, skill-set-possessing and -teaching mentors. Case in point, while I was writing this chapter, an e-mail arrived in my inbox. It was titled "how to get more high fee cases in your office." Hmm, sounds like this guru really cares about your patients. It's all about the money to this guru. We need to root out that type of marketing.

To the starving chiropractor, that marketing may seem like salvation, however, it may be salvation disguised like a wolf in sheep's clothing. Finding a properly equipped mentor is the answer. The mentor must possess the skill set to grow with you over the long haul.

CHAPTER 4

How to Virtually Guarantee Failure in Chiropractic Practice

"I have failed many times, and that's why I am a success."

—Michael Jordan

Yes, I know the title of this chapter is highly negative and depressing, but I thought a title such as this would guarantee that you would pay close attention to the information, so let's dig in.

There is a theory in chiropractic that will virtually guarantee your failure in practice. I call it the shiny magic-bullet theory of success. This theory does not work, never worked over the long haul, and simply makes the salesmen and those who teach personality-dependent practice techniques very, very rich.

Let's look at the largest debacle that's likely hit chiropractic in the past 50 years: the decompression practice. I remember it like it was yesterday. Seminars were everywhere. Equipment manufacturers were bringing new tables to the market with lightning speed. Credit cards were smoking hot from the activity. Lots and LOTS of money was made by manufacturers of the decompression machines. Everyone was looking to strike it rich by going after cash-paying patients. Many docs were unknowingly fraudulently billing insurance companies for decompression by simply doing what they were told in seminars. Chiropractors were placing newspaper ads in record numbers. Patients were flooding into offices as a result of the ads.

Then the ads stopped working and the audits ramped up. Huge lease payments for these machines were unable to be paid back. Chiropractors went out of business in record numbers like never before.

For the uninitiated, decompression is a fantastic modality for patients who have disc problems or specific types of vertebral arthritis. The decompression mania started with some ads in our chiropractic trade journals touting individuals who went from broke to making money hand over fist in record time. A number of manufacturers were involved.

Chiropractors would respond to the advertisements and then show up at seminars where the amazing benefits of the decompression machines were touted. Often, free plane tickets were even offered. Please understand, I'm a huge believer in decompression machines, having seen and experienced the results firsthand. They perform nearly miraculous changes on people who likely couldn't have been helped by any other means than perhaps surgery, which carries its own boatload of risks. So just to get this on record, I think that in the long term, every chiropractor should ultimately be able to offer decompression to those patients who truly can benefit from its application. The caveat here is that a chiropractor should be able to simply write a check for an inexpensive decompression machine rather than sign on the dotted line for a grossly overpriced apparatus that, although it may look like the space shuttle, has benefits that are no different than the inexpensive machines.

I distinctly remember sitting in one of these seminars in 2004 with both my father, Mike Tomshack, who was my director of marketing for my four clinics, and Dr. Rob Prewitt, who is a phenomenally gifted clinician and businessman who owns four clinics himself. We were all sitting in the seminar when the salesman took the stage and began touting the benefits of the decompression machine. Dr. Prewitt and I both knew considerably more about compliance issues than most other chiropractors on the planet, and we knew that what was being explained was highly illegal. Basically, the audience was instructed that this machine could be used on patients with problems and then those services could be billed to insurance companies under a host of different codes. This was 100% illegal then, (and now) and we knew it.

So when the manufacturer's reps were done with their road show, Dr. Rob and I approached them and quoted the regulations that they were violating through their teachings. We told them blatantly that the chiropractors purchasing this equipment and utilizing their coding instructions would likely lose their licenses for following that advice. The reps shrugged it off as if we were morons. I'll never forget that day. In the end, what we predicted was exactly what happened.

At that event, chiropractors were literally lining up to spend obscene amounts of money on grossly overpriced decompression machines. In many cases, they were using financing companies to write the paper for the purchase of this equipment. Now understand, many of these chiropractors could not afford this equipment; nor could they afford the payments if they were leasing it. The decision to purchase or lease these machines would come to haunt many of the buyers.

So as time went on and the marketing materials they were given ceased to work, these doctors were left with absolutely huge monthly lease payments or bank payments on this equipment. Before long, chiropractors were going under at a record pace. Warehouses were becoming full of repossessed machines. You could buy a virtually brand-new and unused piece of equipment for pennies on the dollar in no time at all.

And in our first year of franchising HealthSource, we actually brought on a franchisee that had what he called a "decompression practice"." First of all, there is no such thing as a "decompression practice". Decompression is merely one modality to help care for our patients, and nothing else. You don't now or ever attempt to build a practice on a single modality. It is tantamount to both stupidity and certain failure, but many of the chiropractors sitting in these seminar audiences bought the tale lock, stock, and barrel. They converted their practices from chiropractic practices to "decompression practices" in record numbers. Initially, many of them found success, but, as I mentioned above, the success soon wore off the minute the marketing materials began to lose their effectiveness. And here's a key: marketing always loses its effectiveness at some point in time. Always.

So back to this franchisee we brought on in 2006. He claimed he knew that the era of the "decompression practice" was dead. He wanted to build a healthy practice around chiropractic instead of just a machine. I believed him. Our COO, Brian Dugger, also believed him. Understand that when this franchisee came on board, he would go into his office only a couple of hours every single week to "sell" his new patients on a very high-priced decompression program. He would then leave and go play golf the rest of the week while the patients received treatment under his license while he was not even in the clinic. For those of you who don't know, this is 100% illegal and equates to "go directly to jail." While he said he would change his ways and become compliant immediately, he didn't.

When we confronted him on it and told him we could not allow any type of illegal activity in our franchise family, he simply stated that he was going to run his decompression practice as it was for as long as possible until they shut him down. How crazy is that? We cut him loose immediately and went our separate ways. I have no idea what happened to this doctor, nor do I wish to find out. It's best to keep negative energy at bay.

So, chasing a shiny magic bullet to save your practice is insanity personified. Shiny new pieces of equipment don't save practices. Sound chiropractic and business principles save practices. Evolving your care so your patients receive the very best level of care humanly possible at a fair fee is necessary. As the late, great Jim Rohn stated many times, to be successful and to thrive, you must evolve. Systematizing your practice is absolutely necessary in this complicated day and age. Chiropractors must stop looking at the next shiny magic bullet, decompression machine-like savior, cold-laser machine, magic foot water bath, nutritional supplement, or marketing gimmick to save their practices. It's all fool's gold. A great practice is built on a solid foundation of ethical systems. This is something we *all* are capable of building!

We've seen the same thing happen with highly overpriced cold-laser therapy as in the decompression debacle. This is just the same old pig with different lipstick on it, and some chiropractors fall victim to the allure. The equipment manufacturers are banking on it. It must stop.

As I stated earlier in this book, cold- laser therapy can and, in my opinion, may have a place in building a sound chiropractic practice. And it does for one reason: because it may be able to help answer the question of "what's best for the patient?" However, it is palliative in nature, and is NOT a cure-all. In my opinion, patients should be transitioned to active care as quickly as possible.

This is the question we ask each and every one of our HealthSource family members to ask themselves each and every time they approach a patient, whether it's for the first time or any visit thereafter. Always approach that patient with a clean mind and a clean thought process. Then simply ask yourself, "What's best for the patient?" Next, determine a course of action at that time to simply, efficiently, and ethically answer that question. If cold laser is part of the answer, then so be it. If not, that's fine too. But find the right answer each and every time.

Curious what the newest shiny magic bullet is? Simply, flip open your nearest chiropractic trade journal and read the advertisements. It's never-ending. I would challenge you that as you read each advertisement, ask yourself if the product or service seriously and correctly answers the question of "What's best for the patient?" You'll be a bit disappointed, as I am, each and every time. Once in a while, you will find an ad that attempts to answer the question. Those are the advertisers to which you should pay attention. Please, ignore the rest.

The main problem with the shiny magic-bullet theory of success is that it diverts you from the real problem in your practice, which is you. When you are constantly chasing the next distraction, you are destined to lead a life of frustration and highs and lows. Thoreau said it best when he stated, "Most men lead quiet lives of desperation." I challenge you not to live such a life. I challenge you to look for answers, not gimmicks. As Jim Rohn stated—I paraphrase—to achieve success, work harder on yourself than on your business.

CHAPTER 5

The Biggest Curse of All:
The Personality-Dependent Practice

*"The first method of estimating the intelligence of a
ruler is to look at the men he has around him."*

—Niccolo Machiavelli

Please go back and reread the introductory quote to this chapter.
Think about it. Have you applied this to the team you have in
your office and the people you spend time with outside of the office?

The Personality-Dependent Practice is my favorite topic because it
leads to the largest source of frustration and burn out in chiropractic. It always has, and it always will. I love this topic because a cure
exists. Until HealthSource came on the scene, no one had a viable
and long-term solution. Most weren't even aware of the problem.
What they were aware of was that they were becoming increasingly
unhappy and disillusioned, and that's a shame, because it does NOT
have to occur.

So, let me describe a personality-dependent practice (PDP). To boil it down to its simplest essence, a personality-dependent practice is one in which the doctor cannot unplug himself at will without a corresponding drop in patient visits or clinic income. This means that if the doctor wants to simply leave early and go watch his daughter's softball game, he cannot. The clinic will sink without him, including loss in patient volume and clinic income. Okay, so this is probably totally confusing and confounding to you as you read this.

"How the heck does that happen?" you ask.

To begin with, you must understand that if you have a personality-dependent practice, you don't have a business you have a job. Worse, you're actually punching a time clock.

I'll get to how to structure a practice that is non-personality dependent shortly. In the meantime, please indulge me while I describe the revelation that occurred in my life when I realized I had built a jail.

Quite a number of years ago, I had built a hugely successful practice. It was Huge. I was rolling along, taking care of a lot of patients. I didn't have an associate. I did have a staff. I was seeing a lot of patients, to the tune of an average of 175 a day.

If memory serves, it was a Friday and I had just beat my personal best for the amount of patients seen in one day by me, which does not include family or staff. The number at that time was 204 patients in the day. (Did I mention I was exhausted? Did I mention I went home a tad angry? Did I mention that on that day, I had no desire to break that record ever again?)

I went home and I actually was not in a good mood after breaking my personal record. I knew my patients were receiving excellent care, because they were referring other patients in like crazy and they all got better. It was an amazing environment, but I still wasn't jazzed up.

For me, seeing 204 patients in one day was highly unrewarding. I realized that I had built myself a hamster wheel on which I was running my butt off, with no end in sight. I didn't have a solution yet, but I knew that something was wrong.

Shortly thereafter, something occurred in my life which really drove it home and was the impetus, the catalyst, for enormous change in my life. I'm grateful it occurred.

It was a Thursday evening. My oldest child, Shannon, who was about six at the time, was on a softball team. I'm a baseball player at heart and I wanted nothing more than to get to that game and see my daughter play ball. I was fired up that afternoon.

So I finished up my last patients as fast as I could, knowing that Shannon's game was starting. I finished up with the last patient, jumped in my car, and drove the three miles to the softball field. To this day, I even remember where I parked the Jeep.

I spotted the bleachers on the opposite side of the baseball diamond. It looked like the game was between innings, and I decided to jog across the outfield as quickly as possible so I wouldn't miss a play. Honestly, even if it was in the middle of an inning I probably would have been fine running across the field—how many six year olds are hitting it that far?—but the point is, I was so excited to watch my daughter play that I took off on a dead sprint.

I bolted across the grass and rounded the right field fence when almost out of nowhere a large monster of a man shoved his big beefy hand in my face, stopping me dead in my tracks. It was Mike, the star player's dad. Mike and I were friends: we went to high school together and even played on the same varsity baseball team, but he was big and athletic enough to go on and play four years of Division I college football, so standing in front of me like that was a cause for concern.

"Chris, where you been?" he asked.

I told the truth. "I just finished up work, taking care of patients. What's going on with the game?"

Mike said, "No, I mean, where've you been?"

At this point, I got it. He was basically telling me I was late, so I asked, "What's going on with the game?"

He told me it was the bottom half of the last inning and I'd managed to miss basically the entire game. In that short discussion, Mike managed to make me feel like crap by pointing out the truth. He let me know that while I'm working, I'm failing to participate in Shannon's life; I'm failing to be present, to be a good dad. Shannon could look in the stands and see the parents of the other kids present, but her dad wasn't there; her Dad was at the office, adjusting patients. Wow, talk about a kick in the teeth.

I knew something had to change right then and there. I just wasn't sure what to do. I felt trapped. I had built a hugely financially and clinically successful practice from which I couldn't escape. I had built a jail. It was soft and comfortable, but it was a jail, nonetheless. It hit me like a ton of bricks. There had to be a solution.

I didn't want to be "that dad" who was so driven to be financially successful that I became essentially an absentee father. That's not success. I think that's a failure. I decided that I was going to figure out how to actually be a participant in Shannon's life and not miss her activities. The work began.

Before I tell you what I did, I have to tell you that if you're a fan of "open adjusting," you will never have a life outside of your practice, ever. That is the ultimate personality dependent practice model promulgated by the outdated teachings of today, so if you have an open-adjusting concept, your first task is to get rid of that brontosaurus right quick. Let me explain why.

In an open-adjusting office, every single activity revolves around the doctor. He becomes an actor onstage performing for a crowd. This type of office is built totally for the convenience of the doctor without regard for the patient. When you look at it, you can see that it's a model whose time has come and gone.

As long as everything revolves around the doctor while he is in the practice, the doctor will never escape the confines of the walls of that clinic as long as it is open and seeing patients, so although the clinic can be financially successful, it's 100% dependent upon the personality of the doctor onstage.

Open-adjusting concept aside, virtually every chiropractor on the planet has a personality-dependent practice. It doesn't matter if you're putting patients in adjusting rooms or not. What matters are the processes and systems involved, if any exist at all.

Over the years, I've met some enormously successful doctors. Most recently, a couple of doctors flew in to discuss how HealthSource could fit into their long-term goals. These guys are successful. I mean really successful. Huge numbers of new patients come in every single month, and they are busy in multiple clinics. They are likely the envy of all the other doctors in their area. The enormous challenge is that they've built their empire so that it is based 100% on their personalities being in the clinic at all times, so the three of us discussed the simplest of systems that would need to be implemented for them to begin to extricate themselves from their rabbit fur-lined jail cell. Quite frankly, it scared them. They worried that the numbers would fall.

It's not that the implementation steps are hard, because they're not. I contend that success is simple. It's not easy, but it is simple. These docs seemed quite reticent to take ownership of what needed to be done. I told them the truth, and the truth is that if they can't take the simplest of steps, the HealthSource system will never work for them because they've got their feet firmly entrenched in concrete. This caused them to take pause and hopefully made them both think very hard.

They wanted in. I believed that HealthSource is likely not for them. Not until we are all convinced that they will implement correctly should we decide to move forward. It was the right decision.

So I ask you: Do you have a personality-dependent practice? If you leave your practice at will, do the patient visits and income remain the same or even grow? Can you plug and unplug yourself at will from patient care and the practice continues to hum along?

When I finally made the switch to a practice that was no longer dependent upon my personality, the practice actually grew. It grew a lot. It grew into one of the single largest clinics in the entire country in short order. For that to occur in your practice, you MUST be able to finally let go of the ultra-tight-fisted control issues that many DCs have regarding empowering and teaching others on their teams to make decisions and run with the ball. Unfortunately, this is a step most DCs are unwilling to take. That's a shame, because it's a step to freedom and autonomy. Not to make this decision is a decision in and of itself to remain stuck. If nothing changes, nothing changes.

But understand this: Others on the team finally being allowed to blossom and actually take ownership in the running of the clinic does not mean the doctor can simply leave and play golf all day long. To the contrary, the doctor's role begins to shift into that of a real leader and manager as opposed to a full-time clinician. Everyone grows under this model, and, best of all, the patients receive exceptional care at all times.

The team must be empowered to take ownership in what occurs each day, to make decisions and be held accountable for those decisions. As you move your patients away from passive care and into much more effective active care, your team (when applicable) provides the active care, freeing up the doctor to adjust and communicate and lead more. Everyone wins, especially the patients.

With the patients spending more time with the team for active care, that begins to take the dependence off the doctor's personality. Once this transition is made, it's now possible to bring on an associate doctor and get them trained correctly, thus allowing even more freedom for the owner-doctor.

As the team and associate(s) are trained weekly and held to high standards with performance measured, they become more valuable and should be compensated accordingly. Everyone wins!

CHAPTER 6

The 7-Pillar Solution

"Chance favors the prepared mind."

—Louis Pasteur

The first five chapters of this book held some very important information. Some of it may have irritated you. That was not the intent. The intent was to share with you the truth as I see it and the current realities of the chiropractic profession. Solutions to success in the New Profession are abundant, but it is also uncommon to see these solutions in action and being used correctly. Before delving into what it takes to really be a success in the New Profession, I thought it highly prudent for you to have a firm grasp on exactly what does not work anymore and, most importantly, why it no longer works.

As I've stated numerous times before, the rules have changed regarding operating a successful clinic. Few chiropractors know that the rules have changed. Even fewer have mastered them. This is the reason why chiropractic is currently in a constriction mode rather than an expansion mode. When chiropractic is in constriction mode, fewer people are receiving the often miraculous benefits from state-of-the-art, patient outcome-driven chiropractic care. Then it becomes sort of a closed-loop cycle and entropy sets in. This is not good. This must be reversed. The trend can be reversed only by truly understanding the New Profession so *you* can build a hugely successful clinic serving many, many people.

There was a time when chiropractors simply had to graduate and hang out a sign, and in walked new patients. This isn't happening anymore. Today, when, five years after graduation, approximately 50% of all graduates are no longer in the chiropractic industry whatsoever, the rules must be explained carefully to all chiropractors, young and old. Unless you want to be one of those statistics, let's talk about change: what it is and how you accomplish it. Chiropractic's future depends on your success. Your success depends on your patients' success in obtaining complete healing with a transition into real wellness care. Own your responsibility in this equation. Own it and construct a great practice with incredible results!

To begin with, chiropractors should do what we do best, and nothing more. For this to occur, our teams have to be trained impeccably well. We have to spend and invest a great deal of time and resources to further educate, train, and develop ourselves as individuals and leaders before we can ever begin to empower others on our teams to lead as well, so we must begin by working on ourselves and on our clinical, professional, and personal growth.

Many chiropractors often find this a real kick in the teeth the first time this is explained to them, because, like so many others, when they received doctoral degrees, they think they have finally "arrived." I liken earning a doctoral degree to earning a black belt in martial arts. To me, both mean similar things, namely, that you have demonstrated a base level of expertise in a discipline to earn your degree or rank. From this point forward, the real learning takes place. However, what I see in practice oftentimes is contrary to what should be occurring. That is, the chiropractor gets his degree and assumes he or she has arrived and can now simply practice. As I've mentioned before, I contend that if a doctor is practicing the same way he did when he graduated, that doctor is already woefully obsolete, even if he just graduated the previous year. With the rate at which advances are being made today, it is tantamount to malpractice to not stay 100% current on what is most effective for our patients. This is only part of the personal development I mentioned a short while ago, however; it is merely the clinical aspect. Then there are the mechanics involved. Everything else is related to personal growth.

In HealthSource, we term this working on our personal daily disciplines. We teach that every doctor must inculcate a set of personal daily disciplines that he or she should never veer far from, except to evolve those disciplines. For example, let me describe my morning daily disciplines.

 I wake up early—, earlier than most. Before getting out of bed, I gently flex and extend my foot and ankle to get the blood pumping and to fully awaken my body and mind. I think thoughts of gratitude, listing out things I'm grateful for in my life. Then I get up and walk to my closet, grab a handful of amino acids, walk to the sink, grab some water, and slug them down. Then I shave. While shaving, I read and focus on my goals and affirmations and the 10 secrets to success. Then I put on some workout clothes. Conspicuously absent is any mention of the TV or newspaper.

Then it's off to the pantry for a quick protein shake, always rice- or egg-based in nature. I consume no gluten or dairy and haven't in years. Depending on the day, I either jump in the car and drive three miles to the gym for a high- intensity weight- training program or head down the stairs to my personal workout room for either cardio or a different style weight-training day.

I love my personal workout room. It's a mini gym complete with mirrored walls and stenciled affirmations on every wall. I can't help but feel good about walking into and out of this room. While working out, I will typically listen to a personal-development book on

CD so I can work on my mind and body and, often, spirit all at once. I'm programming myself for mental and physical success for the day to come. Immediately after my workout, it's time for breakfast.

I'm a firm believer in eating to live, not living to eat. My food choices typically reflect this philosophy, so for breakfast, I usually grab the Vita-Mix and begin filling it up. Often, I'll start with 1-½ cups of filtered water, ½ cup steel-cut oats (gluten-free), 20 to 30 grams of rice- or egg-based protein, ½ cup of coconut milk, 1 tablespoon of coconut oil (extra-virgin), 2 cups of organic spinach, one head of organic broccoli, 2 organic carrots, and 2 tablespoons of flaxseed. Often, I'll add some arugula, kale, and mixed greens. Then the Vita-Mix is switched to high for about a minute to totally grind everything up. Then down the hatch it goes. After that, I walk over to my supplement cabinet and grab my morning supplements.

My morning disciplines do not stop there. I quickly jump in the shower, finishing off on cold to stimulate the immune system. I then dress, jump in the car, and drive the 3.5 miles to my office. As soon as I get to work, I meditate for 15 to 20 minutes to completely get my mind right for the day. Then it's time for the morning huddle with my team at 8:30 AM. This is when we stretch and I play a hand in helping everybody else get their minds right for the day. Then I spend the first two hours of every morning on the most demanding and creative work on my itinerary. Our minds are freshest and most creative in the morning, at least for most of us, and so to waste that time reading e-mail, surfing the Web, or doing menial tasks is a complete waste of time and talent.

During the first two and sometimes three hours of the morning, I do my work using the "burning 20s." This means that I set a timer for 20 minutes and work without any distractions for 20 minutes. Then I take a 10-minute break from all work activity, even if I'm in midsentence. The process then repeats. These are my morning disciplines. They do not vary, because they work. That being said, I am not opposed to trying new things to constantly keep my morning disciplines as effective and as tight as possible. This is a winning combination. What are your morning disciplines?

Earlier in this chapter, I mentioned that every chiropractor should do what we do best, and nothing more. For this to reasonably occur, you must be extricated from a personality-dependent practice. We must always remember that everything we do should be designed to deliver better patient outcomes. That's what it's all about. It's not about the numbers, the adjustments, or the number of new patients. It's about patient outcomes. To place your focus on anything else is to chase fool's gold yet again. Remember, it's always about the patients and what's best for them. For you to give your very best to your patients, you must give your very best to yourself first. This means that long-term practice success is predicated upon you taking care of yourself and continuing to grow and evolve as a human being first and as a clinician second.

Indulge me for a moment while I describe the rest of my day. My mentors have taught me that for us to be highly effective and efficient, we must carefully compartmentalize each and every day. For instance, I mentioned that the first two hours of the business day are for creative tasks only, such as writing this book. The rest of my day is blocked into 30-, 60-, or 120-minute segments devoted to such tasks as communications (phone and e-mail), meetings (in person and digital), team development, franchise owner contact, and review of business. The last hour is for any unplanned tasks that need to be handled today or for carryover from the preceding topics.

By carefully compartmentalizing my day, I'm able to accomplish much, much more in one day than the typical person often accomplishes in a week. You may see it as being rigid. I see it as moving closer toward my potential, which I view as one of my main missions in life. As one of my first mentors in chiropractic told me years ago, show me a good pool player, and I'll show you a wasted life.

Before I get into the seven pillars of the solution, I want to leave you with one thought that was taught to me by Michael Gerber: You should always build your practice as if it were designed to be a franchise even though you will very likely not start a franchise.

Why? If you build your practice as if it were to become the prototype for a franchise, you will build and use systems instead of making yours a personality-dependent clinic. Mom-and-pop shops are personality dependent, even the successful ones. A real business runs on systems so the owner can plug him- or herself in and out at will. That's the key.

Okay, let's move on to the seven pillars of the solution to practice success in the New Profession.

CHAPTER 7

Patient Care is EVERYTHING

"What we are we repeatedly do. Excellence, then, is not an act, but a habit."

—Aristotle

Here is a personal challenge: Open up any one of the chiropractic trade journals right now and take a look at all the ads promoting services and products of all kinds. Go ahead and read them. Now assemble all those advertisements into two distinct piles. Into pile number one, stack all the ads that are touting how each particular service or product will help you build your practice and earn railcar loads of cash in record time, all the while requiring minimal work from you. In pile number two, stack all the ads that describe how using these products or services will help you to deliver the absolute best possible care for your patients so that your patients can achieve their health goals. Now compare the two piles.

I'm betting you're pretty much blown away right now because almost every single one of the ads will fall into pile number one. It's as if the advertisers today don't give a hoot about what's best for the patient being treated. It's all about the money, period. It's not the 1990s anymore, and this kind of rubbish must be rooted from our profession. It's cheesy, unprofessional, and pathetic. Patient care is everything. Every decision you make concerning your practice should pass the basic litmus test of "what's best for the patient."

Here's personal challenge number two: Jump in the car and take a drive, stopping at all the chiropractic offices you encounter. Pop in and ask for a quick tour to see what types of services are being provided to their patients. I'll wager well over 90% of the clinics are almost identical in scope. You'll find an adjusting table or two, one or two electrical stimulation machines placed somewhere in the vicinity of a roller table, and a hydrocollator situated on a table somewhere. You might be able to locate an exercise ball somewhere in a dusty corner. This is what I call 1990s-style chiropractic; it's some sort of weird time warp in which many docs find themselves self imposed. High tech and patient outcomes-driven, it ain't.

Chiropractic 1990s style is old school and needs to be evolved. The evolution already exists, so the question you're caught asking yourself right now is "If I'm not using roller tables, e-stim, and hot packs, what the heck am I supposed to be doing in addition to adjusting my patients?"

The answer is simple. Use what works best. That means you need to pay attention to all the scientific advances affecting healthcare today. Most of the early pioneers in chiropractic were constantly looking for evolutions in both the detection and diagnosis of patient problems as well as for new and better treatment to eliminate the problems. We must continue their great work, because the quest will never end. Advances are always being made and will continue to be made as long as chiropractic exists. It's incumbent upon us to remain relevant and avant-garde.

Don't look to the equipment manufacturers for what's best. These guys are merely peddling their wares, looking for new and different ways to get you to buy their shiny magic bullets to practice success. By now, I hope you sincerely realize there are no shiny magic bullets to success, and that if you rely on others to deliver such magic bullets, you're destined for a life of desperation and mediocrity. Is that really what you set out to achieve when you graduated?

Now you're faced with the question of, "Well, how the heck am I supposed to know what's working the best if I'm not hiring gurus to explain it to me?" You must read. You must scour the periodicals in the literature and the newest books to see for yourself what is currently being proven to be the best. The trade journals will not have the newest information. These are, by definition, trade journals. Mentorship is a concrete must-have tool in your arsenal for you to stay up to date.

At this point, I'm going to help you out. The remaining content of this chapter is going to describe what is proven to work best today to not only deliver the very best in patient care but also help you build a highly successful practice in the New Profession. What works today will most certainly change in the coming months and years. You CANNOT remain stagnant.

What I'm about to share may offend you. I hope it doesn't. It will challenge your beliefs. It will challenge how you take care of patients. What I do care about is that your eyes are opened past dogma and into reality and searching for the truth. I care that all patients receive the very best care available. Let's implant reality and critical thinking. As Aristotle said, "It is the mark of an educated mind to entertain a thought without accepting it." So let's begin.

The first thing to analyze is your chiropractic technique. This is one area in chiropractic in which it is most difficult to help chiropractors; that's because we tend to become highly dogmatic about the way we adjust our patients. It's almost as if the day we graduate, the learning in chiropractic technique stops. Please, please do not let that happen in your mind. In what other health discipline does this anomaly occur?

True, we had some absolutely brilliant pioneers in the chiropractic profession over the years blaze beautiful trails in furthering advances in chiropractic technique, but it doesn't stop there. We must endeavor to constantly improve their advancements and our technique. The chiropractic colleges teach a nice basic package of adjusting skills. The challenge is that many of the techniques they teach are fairly old. Yes, those techniques have helped millions of people, but the search for truth and knowledge didn't end with the discovery of these techniques.

Many changes and advances in evolutions continue to happen in the field of chiropractic technique each year. If you have not taken coursework in the advances of chiropractic technique, you're behind the eight ball. In other words, you're outdated and becoming obsolete, and you will be left behind!

When I refer to chiropractic-technique seminars, I'm not talking about technique that was discovered decades ago. I'm talking about taking classes in the newest advances in chiropractic technique, those which are well researched and scientifically validated. A point of clarification is probably in order here: Detoxification foot baths are not chiropractic technique. Nutrition is not chiropractic technique. I'm talking about actual chiropractic adjustments on the spine or other articulations. I'll get to nutrition and soft-tissue technique shortly because those are highly important as well.

If you wish to remain state of the art, you must advance your technique, and your technique must continually advance throughout your entire career. Think how much fun a trip to the dentist would be if they were still drilling teeth the way they did 60 years ago. We must strive to be the best we can possibly be. The learning never ends.

Let's move on to talk about deep-tissue work. From this point forward, I am going to make the assumption that you are committed to evolving your chiropractic technique and delivering an absolutely superior adjustment to your patients.

Muscle imbalances and asymmetries are a primary cause, in addition to trauma, of the skeletal conditions we often encounter. To ignore the imbalances and asymmetries is tantamount to malpractice, all while keeping your head buried in the sand.

For years, chiropractors assumed that offering massage in their clinics by licensed massage therapists would address these issues. It does not. In fact, classic massage does very little, if anything, to address asymmetries and imbalances within the soft-tissue structure. What is proven to work the best today is what I call functional deep-tissue work.

Functional deep-tissue work is so much more than simply old-school trigger-point work. Functional deep-tissue work actually gets in the soft tissue and begins to strip away the years of adhesions and fibrotic deposition that have occurred as a result of overuse—asymmetries and imbalances contained within the patient's musculoskeletal structure. In other words, if the work isn't painful, it simply isn't effective.

Functional deep-tissue work involves taking a muscle through its entire range of motion while applying either constant pressure to the appropriate area or systematically applying pressure to the muscle belly or the origin or insertions of the muscles and tendons during specific periods of movement to help break through adhesions and allow full range of motion to return as the body heals itself.

Many newer schools of thought and procedures are being taught today that are light years ahead of what was taught even 10 years ago. I encourage a non-dogmatic approach in exploring these advances, as many, if not all, of these techniques have some efficacious validity. Much like studying several martial arts will make you a much better martial artist, combining the best of what these systems teach is the best approach.

At HealthSource, this is exactly what we do. We continually search out each year the best advances in functional deep-tissue work and then certify all of our clinics across the country in their usage. This keeps all the doctors continually current on what works best for the patient. It evolves to some extent every single year. The patients win again!

What works best for the patient in conjunction with functional deep-tissue work is functional therapeutic taping. After conducting much research, I know that the Rock Tape methodology is the most therapeutically efficacious taping system that exists today.

The Rock Tape method has built upon and evolved previous schools of thought with therapeutic tape; in addition; it has built a superior tape. We've tested all the tapes, and universally, Rock Tape comes out on top. If you want to truly help your patients recover faster, Rock Tape must be on your list of systems to learn.

I no longer practice, since running HealthSource consumes all of my available time, but let me relate a short story. Last year, my oldest son's baseball team had a varsity game. The star shortstop of the team was at the plate and was struck by a fastball right on his elbow…right on the bony prominence. He went down like a ton of bricks. The trainer came running out, and the player was carried off to the dugout. About 10 minutes later, the boy's father came and sat down next to me, where he had been prior to the incident, and so I asked him how his son was doing.

He told me that his son's elbow was completely swollen and he was unable to move his arm. The trainer had put ice on the elbow, put the entire arm in a sling, removed him from baseball for a minimum of two weeks, and had already, from the dugout, booked an appointment with the orthopedic surgeon for the next morning. I thought this a bit draconian, given the circumstances and my knowledge.

I merely asked the father if he'd like for me to get his son back to playing baseball in about three days. He nodded his head emphatically and looked bewildered. I told him to bring his son over to my house after the game and I would take a look at the arm.

The father and son were so excited about getting healing that they beat me to my house after the game. The boy's arm was in a sling, and his elbow was tightly wrapped in an elastic bandage while a huge bag of ice sat precariously on top of the elbow. I removed the ice and bandage and examined the arm. It was grotesquely swollen, and the range of motion was extremely restricted, to about zero. Other than acute soft-tissue damage, I could detect no other injury.

I taped the boy's arm using the newest taping procedures for therapeutic taping and told him to expect 90%–95% of the swelling to be gone the following morning. I told him not to throw the baseball the next day but that within 48 hours, he would be able to gently throw the ball. On the third day, Monday, he should be able to play in the game. I asked the father to call me the following morning to let me know how his son's arm was doing.

I received a call about nine in the morning. The swelling was nearly 100% gone. The boy was able to move his arm virtually 100% and was asking to go outside to test his arm by throwing a baseball. I told him NO and to do exactly what I had told them the night before.

Suffice it to say that three days post injury (Monday), he was starting in the baseball game. No appointment was necessary with the orthopedic surgeon. What I neglected to tell you was that a reporter from the newspaper had been present at the game and had witnessed the severity of the incident. He was blown away that the boy could start three days later, so he felt compelled to write a very large article on the whole incident. Just think what that would have done if I were still practicing and had a practice to promote!

The next procedure that is giving outstanding benefits to patients is functional therapeutic exercise. This is not the old-school exercise protocols you most likely learned. It is also not the old-school exercise protocols most seminars are teaching. This is the newest stuff, far superior to the old-school methods.

Functional exercise involves multiple muscle groups moving through various planes of motion involving multiple angles of movement. In other words, you're not doing bicep curls!

For directly addressing your patients' muscle imbalances and asymmetries, there is nothing better than functional exercise efficaciously applied to remove these impediments to health while establishing much better strength and symmetry.

Next up is functional stretching. Here again, we're not talking about the old-school stretching that your high school football or volleyball coach had you doing prior to practice. Throw that old-school stuff out with the bathwater, which is about how useful it really is. And while you're at it, stop telling your patients to stretch before engaging in their exercise programs. What is proven to work is something entirely different.

Functional stretching involves assisted resistance and assistance in taking a muscle through its current perceived end range of motion and gradually increasing the stretch by negating the stretch receptors. One of the schools of thought in this endeavor is PNF stretching. With PNF stretching, you can often accomplish more benefit, more stretching, in a few short weeks than the patient could have achieved in months and months, even years, of classical stretching. The two don't even compare.

Probably the easiest way to begin learning this is to simply take some coursework in PNF stretching as a primer. Yes, you must stay current.

The next critical complement that must be addressed is nutrition. Oh my gosh, is there a ton of misinformation on nutrition. As I discussed earlier in this book, we must feed the injury. If the human body does not have the building blocks for healing to occur, it just doesn't happen in a complete fashion. Nutrition is a huge part of those building blocks.

The problem with nutrition today is that most of the supplementation available is synthetic and therefore not the best option.

Synthetic vitamins CAN cause cancer. I recommend you study the writings and research of Dr. James Chestnut to begin your nutritional education.

Yes, you studied nutrition in college. Kudos to you. However, that was classical nutrition. Now let's learn what really works. As discussed earlier in this book, you begin with the three basic essential supplements and work from there. In a perfect world, the three basic essential supplements would be all that your patients require. One of your most basic missions should be to ensure that your patients are not ingesting any synthetic vitamins, as again, those vitamins can be carcinogenic.

Dr. Chestnut's work is highly researched. He backs up what he says with sound science. We teach our HealthSource family Dr. Chestnut's protocols implicitly. His research shoots arrows through the claims of most of the supplement manufacturers and their hired gurus and shows those claims for what they really are: sales hype.

Your patients deserve much more than just hype. They deserve the best. Start with the three basic essential supplements (nonchemically concentrated omegas, vitamin D, and probiotics) and further your education. Your patients' health depends upon it, as do your health and your family's health.

The last item I want to talk about here as it pertains to evolving your clinical protocols is real wellness care. Throughout chiropractic's history, a lot of the gurus have talked about maintenance care for patients. What they mean by maintenance care is simply having a patient come in at some predetermined time for a chiropractic adjustment, often once per month. I would certainly consider that maintenance care. It is not wellness care.

The baby boomers are turning age 65 to the tune of 10,000 people per day. This generation more than any preceding generation does not want to get, look, or feel old, and it is willing to spend whatever it takes to meet that goal. Baby boomers are spending most of their money currently on junk-based science. You can and should help them.

HealthSource considers real wellness care to consist of a chiropractic adjustment; sound, efficacious nutrition; and other therapeutically necessary additions whenever applicable, all designed to help patients maintain high levels of health. Educational counseling on home exercise and lifestyle are, of course, mandatory.

Now get this: The interim time when a patient should return should be based entirely on the patient's needs. Each patient faces a different set of daily stresses and has different lifestyle challenges depending upon the life he or she lives. We work with our doctors to take a look at all this information and to determine a wellness care program that is best for each patient. There is no one-size-fits-all program that every human being can fit into. That would be outright rubbish and a dogma-based paradigm. Please dispense with this unscientific approach.

America's healthcare crisis is spiraling out of control. Obesity is skyrocketing. Diabetes is going crazy. People are taking far too many drugs. In other words, what America needs is real wellness care. Chiropractors are the perfect doctors to provide this care, but you can provide it only if you are well schooled on what real wellness care is all about. You did NOT receive the information in school.

I challenge you to take a good, hard look at what I've written in this chapter and to determine if you're up to the challenge of providing wellness care to your community, to be the wellness expert in your area. If you're up to that challenge, you shouldn't have any major practice woes. Not only should your patients achieve a much higher level of wellness throughout their lives, but your practice will thrive. In my opinion, this is where chiropractic shines the brightest. Are you up to the challenge? I hope so, because you can do it!

CHAPTER 8

The Compliance Nightmare Is Stalking You!

"Perfection is not attainable, but if we chase perfection, we can catch excellence."

—Vince Lombardi

The quote you just read from Lombardi is extremely relevant as it is applied to compliance in the New Profession. You may wish to go back and reread it.

If you are using travel cards for your documentation, I would suggest that you not spend a dime of the income you are collecting, because you will be paying it back soon. It doesn't matter if you are an all-cash practice, either. Compliance is compliance, period, and you MUST meet the requirements for compliant documentation whether or not you accept insurance. What we are seeing today is a scourge disguised in the name of file audits traveling from chiropractor to chiropractor and destroying them in the process.

I'm going to try really hard not to paint too pretty a picture here, because this stuff is just too damn serious to take lightly. I'm talking to chiropractors who are getting audited and being forced to pay back sums ranging from a few hundred dollars to well over a million dollars. They appeal and they lose, so they appeal again. They lose again. And God help them if they get audited by Medicare or Medicaid, because these two institutions are the 600-pound gorilla that you cannot get off your back, and you will not win.

As a matter of fact, the fastest growing segment of healthcare today is not what you might think. The fastest growing segment in healthcare is third-party auditing firms, which get paid on a percentage of money that they extract from providers by failing providers in audit processes. Does this sound like a conflict of interest to you? It sure does to me.

The audit you will receive may revolve around medical (chiropractic) necessity for the care that was provided to patients, or it may revolve around the quality of the documentation to support the delivery of care to the patients. The bottom line is that your documentation must support the level of care that you provided to every single patient on every single visit. It's as if these auditors are salivating at the prospect of auditing more chiropractors. There's a great reason for this to keep happening, too.

They're auditing more chiropractors because as a whole, the quality of documentation by the chiropractic profession is sadly lacking. Now, before you cry foul, I was not taught how to document properly way back in college, either, but that is no excuse in the eyes of the law and certainly, it is not an excuse in the minds of auditors hellbent on earning their bonuses off the backs of well-intentioned chiropractors and other providers.

Who sets the rules for these auditing companies and their minions to follow? This is an easy one: Medicare. Medicare writes the gold standard by which all insurance companies and auditors derive their processes for determining the medical necessity of the care you've provided your patients as well as the quality of the documentation to support that care. The good news is that all of these Medicare regulations are very easy to find. They're listed on the Medicare website. You just might want to log on and start learning, right quick.

In study after study in state after state, Medicare has clearly told the chiropractic profession that as a whole, our documentation is highly deficient. In one state, Medicare indicated that chiropractic had a 99% failure rate with respect to the quality of documentation. This is sad, and it need not be this way.

So what's a chiropractor to do? For me, I spent tens of thousands of dollars learning how to become compliant. This is just plain unreasonable for the average chiropractor to be able to afford. In fact, a couple of the compliance seminars I've attended blatantly gave inaccurate advice! And because most chiropractors do not yet understand what it takes to be compliant, these audits are absolutely destroying practices.

Let me let you in on a little secret: The minute you get a request for records, a simple request for records, you are essentially undergoing an audit process. You just don't know it yet. This audit process may take only a couple of months, or it may run on into a couple of years, but you are now being investigated. Just about the worst thing you can do is to simply photocopy the records and send them in to the auditors. They are praying this is exactly what you will do, and they attempt to scare you into doing just that by giving you an extremely short deadline. If you simply photocopy your records and send them in, you may be in for a world of pain.

Are you depressed yet? If you are using travel cards, it's time to get out the smelling salts! There is no way in the world you can provide enough quality documentation on a travel card to substantiate your patient receiving any level of care in your office on a date of service. In fact, if any more than one visit can fit on a single sheet of paper, chances are extremely high that you are noncompliant. It's time to get serious before it's too late. Yes, it requires work to learn compliance, and you must have highly competent mentors in this field, especially for when you get a records request.

What I can tell you is that the pace and rate of the audits sweeping chiropractic today will do nothing but increase in the years to come. The auditing industry has become self-sustaining by sinking its teeth into your jugular vein, also known as your income stream.

So you're thinking, "What am I supposed to do? Should I buy one of those electronic medical records programs because they can spit out such a nice, thick narrative report?" Here's a short answer: no.

Frankly, I looked at just about every system of electronic medical records out there for chiropractic and couldn't find one that could pass the level of a Medicare audit. Not one. They all spit out really nice-looking narrative reports, but that's no longer what the auditors are looking for. They've moved on, and in typical fear-driven fashion, hardly anyone has noticed, because everyone is trying to find a program that spits out the cool narrative report. I have. Auditors are looking for the entire trail that led up to an individual specific date of service, and they analyze that trail to look for a series of occurrences to substantiate a specific date of service. A nice glossy narrative does not provide this level of documentation. It merely provides a summary. A summary is not what auditors are looking for at all. They are looking for the minutiae contained in each and every date of service to substantiate every service provided on every occurrence as well as the objective measurements to substantiate continued progress. Absent any of this information, you will fail the audit, regardless of how beautiful the narrative is that you send.

As a matter of fact, at HealthSource, we actually had to work with several companies to design our own electronic medical-records program so that it would be compliant. The average chiropractor down the street can simply not afford this process. It's crazy, but it IS the current reality.

Your mission right now should be to determine how quickly you can become compliant with as little disruption to your business as is humanly possible. You can start with a paper system or an electronic system. To me, it doesn't matter. Eventually, you will be forced over to electronic health records, but that is not yet the case. In the words of one of the compliance experts we've hired numerous times over the years, "When you change your documentation over so that it is now compliant, it makes you look a whole lot less guilty."

The one thing you can never do is add to your notes as if the additional information was made on the date of service that you just altered. That's called fraud. That'll get you a quick trip to your state board. It's not worth it. Don't do it. What you do need to do is become compliant as of today so that all future documentation is compliant. It shows that you have made an honest effort at evolving your documentation skills so they are on par with the skills of all the other providers in the country.

Some of you reading this may be thinking, "But I run an all-cash practice, so this doesn't apply to me." You probably made that statement to yourself with a smug grin on your face. I'd wipe the grin off, because you are 100% wrong. The level of care and subsequent documentation to substantiate the care you provide to patients must be compliant regardless of whether the patient is paying cash or some other institution or entity is paying for that patient's care. It all has to be compliant today. There are no exceptions. NONE. Not even if you're bartering for chickens!

So how do you get compliant? Well, number one, your notes must be in S.O.A.P. format, as indicated on the Medicare website. And just in case you were wondering, that capitalized "O" means "objective." In case you're still confused, objective means reproducible by different examiners. This is termed inter-examiner reliability. In other words, using a great big protractor laid across the shoulders of the patient doesn't pass muster.

This is one of the biggest things missed today in chiropractic: teaching objective measures. Functional outcomes are also necessary. There are many ways to accomplish performing and documenting functional-outcomes assessments. The important thing to remember is they must be objective. In addition, the patient's subjective assessments should also be included. All of this should be accomplished routinely.

How about those re-examinations? Are you re-examining your patients at the correct intervals and for the correct reasons? Are you doing them at all? Did you know you have to perform re-examinations? Do you know how often? Are you now seriously confused?

Here's another little secret: Re-examinations must be performed every 30 days. It doesn't matter if this patient is a maintenance patient or an active-care patient; Re-examinations must be done every 30 days. There is no room for interpretation on this topic.

Third-party payers do not pay for continued care after which the patient is no longer making continued progress. At that point, they must be converted to a cash basis, as it is no longer deemed a covered service. Did you know that? You do now.

Honestly, getting compliant is a very difficult task to do on your own. I recommend that you hire certified coaches to assist you in your educational process. There are just too many detours to get sidetracked on that can take you down the rabbit hole and prevent you from becoming compliant. Especially because the rules are changing with regularity, it pays to have compliance coaches keeping you abreast of everything that is current so that your only real mission is to make sure you are implementing correctly, documenting correctly, and converting patients over to cash pay when it is chiropractically necessary to do so. It will give you incredible peace of mind.

It's also highly important that you employ a qualified individual to regularly review and audit your files to ensure that you maintain high compliance at all times. It's easy to get lazy, especially if you have associates working for you. Documentation must be constantly checked to ensure it is up to all applicable standards.

So, if you are still using travel cards, you need to get busy on this today—but finish this book first so you have a complete list. Perform some research and find a solution for noncompliant documentation before it's too late.

Now, let's continue, because the next chapter is one that is near and dear to my heart, because without it, long-term success is just not sustainable.

Me surfing in Hawaii.

Standing with our Regional Developer Support Team of the Year. From left: Dr. Casey and Courtney Paulsen, Rachelle and Dr. Alan Bergquist.

From left: Dr. Jim Hoven (HealthSource Compliance Officer), Dr. Darin Denamur (owner of two HealthSource offices in North Carolina), and myself at SuperCamp Awards Night.

Dr. Mason Orth (owner of two offices in North Dakota),
and myself at SuperCamp.

Me and my beautiful bride Lisa.

My classic 1972 Nova.

My lovely family. From left: Me, Lisa, Shannon, Chris Jr., and Zack.

CHAPTER 9

Nothing Works Without This...

"Work harder on yourself than on your business."

—Jim Rohn

Mechanics in a practice are important. Without proper mechanics, success will be beyond your grasp at all times, so we're going to talk a lot more about mechanics throughout this book, but before we get to the mechanics part, it's vitally important that you know that mechanics without purpose will only lead to short-term success. To the uninitiated, the success will inexplicably fall apart without truly understanding the "why" behind the "what". To those who already understand this concept, it makes perfect sense. Let me explain.

When given proper instruction in the mechanics of how to run a successful practice, it is certainly possible to begin to achieve a modicum of success. You can even become wildly successful…but it will be short lived. Over the long term, if you rely strictly on mechanics for the catalyst of your success, you will begin to burn out eventually.

It happened to me years ago, and I've seen it happen to thousands of doctors.

Chiropractors are drawn to chiropractic in most cases for far more reasons than just to be in the healing arts or to earn a good income. As a matter of fact, the doctors that I've seen who've pursued chiropractic strictly from a financial- gain aspect have universally ended up making poor decisions that have adversely affected their businesses and their lives. It's because their mission is screwed up. There are plenty of other ways to make a great income that have nothing to do whatsoever with patient care. To choose chiropractic just to make a good income is a very poor decision.

Bluntly, chiropractic is a different kind of business that requires a different kind of individual. It requires an individual who is truly interested in serving others for the right reasons, not to just earn more income. In other words, it's all about the "why" behind what chiropractors do that makes all the difference in the world. And it's this "why" that will ultimately determine whether a chiropractor is successful both clinically and financially.

In my years both of practicing and of mentoring doctors, I've noticed that those doctors who practice with passion and purpose not only have much more fun filling their lives but also earn much better incomes. It's a winning recipe. And hey, who doesn't want to have a happier life? Count me in!

So the trick now is to figure out how to spark the passion for chiropractic deep inside yourself. But you know what? There's actually a step that comes before this one, and that step is to completely (100%) accept personal responsibility for where you currently are in life and where you will ultimately end up in the future.

You may want to reread that last sentence.

Yes, we live in an entitlement society. An entitlement mind-space will thoroughly prevent you from ever achieving success. And what do I mean by an entitlement mind-space? Simple. It means that you look to others for your success. You may even feel that because you spent all the time and money to become a chiropractor, you deserve success.

Successful entrepreneurs banish that thought whenever it rears its ugly, disease-ridden head. I encourage you to do the same thing. It's all about personal responsibility. No one owes any of us anything. We create our lives and destinies.

Where you are today in terms of success or happiness is a direct result of the quality of decisions you have made up to today. The really cool thing is that the decisions you've made in the past, even though they may have been incorrect, should have no bearing whatsoever on the future. Think about that for a minute.

You've got a whole new slate in front of you today. You see, I don't believe there is some giant whiteboard in the sky that has clearly written on it everything that you are going to ever achieve and everything that occurs to you or around you throughout your lifetime. I believe that we've been given free will and free choice to make the decisions that mold our lives. That whiteboard in the sky contains writing for sure, but it's writing that we have put on it ourselves based on the decisions that we have made. I challenge you to make better decisions. The way to make better decisions is to grow ourselves personally. This is key, and it's never-ending.

One of the affirmations that I read myself several times a day contains the statement "I work on personal development daily." Without personal-development work, we stagnate, we don't grow, so the quality of our decisions does not improve. Work on your personal growth, and your decisions will improve. As your decisions improve, your life improves. As your life improves, you have the capacity to help others even more and to a much deeper level, so, as Zig Zigler has stated so many times before, "You can have everything in life that you want if you just give enough other people what they want." This is an absolute keystone for long-term success.

So, start growing yourself today. But now you're asking, "Well, how the heck do I do that?"

How about you get online and order some personal-development books? Start reading them today and never stop. I reserve a minimum of a half hour of reading time every day, and often much more. Without fail, a portion of that time is always dedicated to personal-development materials. It's what works for me. It's what works for those around me. It's what works for my mentors. That's good enough for me! I think it's good enough for you, too.

The next step is to carefully carve your daily personal disciplines into your day. Make them unbending. I mean literally put them into your daily schedule and never schedule over them. By daily disciplines, I'm talking about things such as meditating, reading personal-development books, listening to personal-development books, getting adjusted, getting the proper nutrition, exercising, and sleeping.

Achieving peak efficiency and therefore progress and success demands a great deal of discipline—much more than most people invest in themselves. To pretend it isn't integral is delusional and self-defeating and is a trait of the non-successful. Choose success.

As you begin to explore your own true personal development, it's time to begin to mentor others to help them and support them in their own personal-development journeys. I challenge you to share what you are learning in the genre of personal development with those around you. I do it daily basis in the team huddle that we have every day at 8:30 AM. All of the HealthSource clinics also have an 8:30 AM huddle daily. How?

This is actually quite simple. I take one of the items that I've learned in the preceding 24 hours. Often, it's something I've just listened to on CD on the way to work. I then take a few minutes and explain what it is and the effect it had on me and how I plan to implement it into my life beginning today. To ensure those on my team are also engaged in this process, because I know it will benefit them and make them much more valuable in the long term, I schedule a portion of every team huddle, on a rotating basis, for one team member a day to share something he or she has recently learned regarding personal development. The team member must explain the thing in detail and discuss how it affects his or her life.

Does this sound a tad bit uncomfortable? Of course it does!

Unless you're constantly pushing your boundaries into the area of discomfort, you won't grow. All growth requires some discomfort or pain. Learn to accept it. Learn to embrace it, and learn to expect it daily. This is what winners do.

A huge leader in personal development is John C. Maxwell. I encourage you to read any of the many books that he has authored. He has some pretty profound thoughts on winners. He states that winners have five tendencies that you must incorporate in your life if you want to be a habitual winner:

Winners are passionate about what they do.
Winners value the process of winning.
Winters focus on their strengths and not their weaknesses.
Winners focus on winning on the inside more than the outside.
Winners persist on a path toward success.

The preceding information was from an article that John Maxwell wrote in the February 2013 edition of *Success* magazine. This is a magazine I encourage you to read, as it gives daily information that you can begin to implement into your life so you can begin to be a habitual winner as well.

Please, begin reading and listening to personal-development books and audiobooks. It's a very basic common denominator of high achievers, and it's painless and simple to initiate. Get busy!

CHAPTER 10

The Weekly Training Habit

"It's not the will to win that matters, everyone has that. It's the will to prepare to win that matters."

—Paul "Bear" Bryant

One of the most common questions posed to me by chiropractors outside of HealthSource is "How do I get my staff behind me to help grow my practice?" Well first of all, if you have a staff, you have an infection. I'd stop using the term "staff" today and instead start using the word "team." Words are everything. Words connote specific meanings, feelings, and emotions. Choose your words carefully and start building a team instead of a staff.

A team is a group of people who are "all in, all the time." To build a great team, you must have people with the correct attitude and aptitude.

By and large, chiropractors are little lone rangers fighting their own fights all by themselves while sequestered in their offices. This is a recipe for mediocrity for your entire career. It's what most chiropractors do their *ENTIRE* careers. You must think bigger. You must act bigger. You must have a well-trained team by your side totally aligned with your goals and vision and ready to do whatever it takes to achieve that vision. Before you instantly give a knee-jerk reaction and state, "Yeah, well, that's not really possible now, is it?" hold on, because it's extremely doable.

We're doing it all across America in HealthSource clinics every single day, and you can do it, too. First, you have to be open to the possibility that it can be done. Then you need to know the mechanics of how it is done. Then you must have the self-discipline and personal responsibility to begin the implementation process. Everyone on this planet has that inborn ability to be ultra-successful. Few, however, ever truly dig down deep enough to learn about themselves and improve themselves to a level at which building an enormously successful practice becomes easy.

It's really all about the training. The training must start with you, and it must start immediately. We cannot teach what we do not own and know deep in our cores, in our very essences, so before you begin to start training your team and leading them successfully, you must first train and lead yourself. It always starts with us first.

We've already talked about implementing personal disciplines into your life. This is the first integral step. You really may as well not read any further in this book unless you are willing to initiate and implement personal disciplines in your life. If need be, go back and read that chapter. Then read it again. Training starts with YOU implementing non-negotiable personal disciplines.

So, I'm making the assumption that you have begun to firmly implant and inculcate personal disciplines into your life. Congratulations! Have you considered going gluten and dairy free? Did I mention to you that once I eliminated them both, my allergies totally disappeared? By the way, prior to going away to officer's boot camp when I was 20, the Air Force shot me up with all types of vaccines. I immediately developed terrible seasonal allergies. Going gluten and dairy free changed my life.

Shifting gears, now let's talk about training your team.

Most chiropractors are under the mistaken impression that all that is necessary is to load up your team, attend a motivational seminar by some guru, and it's off to the races! This will never suffice in building a great, well- trained team. Training has to be approached scientifically with a specific purpose and intent and a specific plan of action. Training also never stops.

In HealthSource, we train our teams every single week of the year. For us, it occurs every Tuesday morning from 9:30 AM until 1 PM… every single Tuesday. Yes, you read that right, every single Tuesday.

We have 26 different training modules that we rotate through twice a year. In addition, a live webinar of an hour's duration is put on by our corporate team for our entire franchise family. In other words, training is not boring. It is dynamic and ever-changing, and it is always high energy.

One of the most basic elements you must continually train your team on is communication skills. Everyone reading this book has scripts that he follows throughout his life, most of the time not even realizing he's doing it. The problem is that most of our scripts are pretty much pathetic.

In other words, when a patient gives you a specific objection to following the care plan you just prescribed, you typically have a set answer that you go through. Whether or not you realize it, this is a script.

Back when I was in college at Ohio University, I not only was a business major but was also in the Air Force ROTC program. In ROTC, we were constantly drilled on improving our communication abilities.

My commanders taught me that the real definition of communication is me telling you something and you understanding it as I intended it to be understood. Most of us go through life talking with others and never really giving it a second thought if that person truly understands what we just said; we just keep talking. And as was taught to me by one of my first martial arts instructors, Master Tony Perry, "The empty can rattles the loudest." Give that one a little thought. I think back on this quote at least once a week…and Master Perry taught me this way back in 1988. It's proven accurate. Are you the empty can? If so, let's fill that can up!

Most of us, when communicating with others, can be like that empty can with a rock in it, rattling on and on and on with no regard to whether the other people really understand our messages. I challenge you to stop being an empty can and to instead focus on delivering clear and concise communication to those around you. In other words, seek to be interested and not interesting.

All this being said, training on communication should occur every single week. You should have scripting for virtually every type of patient encounter that can occur in your office on a given day. It should be well thought out. In other words, it starts with the phone. When the phone rings, your team should be trained on how to answer it appropriately and how to handle every occurrence that can potentially be encountered while on the phone with a patient or a prospective new patient. This leaves no room for chance or error.

As a matter of fact, your clinic loses more business week after week as a result of inept phone skills than any other reason. If you truly knew how awful your team is at utilizing appropriate phone skills, it would blow you away. Here's a challenge: Have a friend call your office. Have her pose as a potential new patient asking specific questions. Make sure you record the call. Now go shut yourself away in a dark room and listen to the recording. If you are seized with the urge to kill someone, go to the gym and work out instead! Maybe go run five miles. I've done many mystery calls over the years, and rare has been the occasion when someone truly has been trained well enough to effectively and efficiently handle any and all challenges and objections thrown at him over the phone and do so professionally. When it does occur correctly, it's the sign of a well-trained team and a good leader. You need this component in yourself and in your team.

Scripting goes a whole lot further than just answering the phone. You should carefully prepare scripting for virtually every encounter that can take place inside the office. You should have scripting for when a new patient enters the office, for when an existing patient enters the office, for examination processes, for report of findings processes, and for communication that occurs on each subsequent visit as well as on reexaminations…even for wellness visits.

When you and your team drill, train, and rehearse your scripting procedures every week, you all become much more valuable and much more professional. It also will lead to predictable results, with the most important one being improved patient care because the patient understands why they are there on every given visit so they maintain their care plan to closure. Are you prepared to engage in this activity? Do you really want to be successful, or would you rather just complain that it's too hard to be successful and simply state that the reason the others are successful is because they are lucky or they live in a better town? That is all rubbish. If you want success, do what the winners do. Winners train constantly.

I was reading a story just the other day about professional basketball player LeBron James. It turns out LeBron heard that one of his teammates, instead of taking the bus from the hotel to the arena, chose to jog the two miles to the practice facility for extra workout time. Never wanting to be outdone in terms of training by anyone else, LeBron quickly shed his street clothes, put on some workout attire, and joined his teammate in the jog instead of taking the team bus. This is classic LeBron activity: out-work everybody else so you are the best. LeBron is the best. Are you prepared to do what it takes to be the best? You can have excuses or success, but not both. I caution you to choose carefully.

Another topic we often train on at HealthSource is Grand Rounds. Grand Rounds means examining all active- care patient files to ensure that the treatment has been upgraded wherever possible so that the patients are always receiving the absolute best in state-of-the-art care so they get a much deeper and profound healing outcome. It also ensures that you understand if a patient has dropped out of care prematurely so you can take appropriate steps to train so that this happens less and less in the future.

When your practice has evolved to the extent that you now have associates seeing patients as well, it becomes imperative and absolutely necessary that your associate doctors use this Grand Rounds opportunity to carefully explain why they have prescribed a certain plan of care at a specific point in time for all of their patients.   So in a sense, your associate doctors actually defend their care programs for their patients. It's also an opportunity to see how every patient is progressing, since you are no longer seeing all the patients. This gives you a wonderful opportunity to help train your doctors in clinical excellence.

If you are truly giving your patients your best, their care programs will change and upgrade as they heal and improve. To keep your patients on the same care program the entire time is highly antiquated and virtually guarantees sub par outcomes. That's mediocrity. Upgrading treatment programs, when indicated, is what's best for the patient.

Another common topic in our trainings is a motivational themed content component. As Zig Zigler was fond of saying, "People often say motivation doesn't last. Well, neither does bathing- that's why we recommend it daily."

Always provide some form of motivational training and teaching during every training session. Don't just wing this and expect it to be splendid. You'll be wasting your time and, most importantly, wasting your team's time. Treat training professionally. Put the time in and get it done right.

In our daily morning huddles, one team member a day is assigned to prepare a motivational or educational teaching moment. The team member knows well in advance and puts the time in to do it correctly so the moment has meaning, purpose, and intent. All trainings should have thorough preparation beforehand so that when it comes to execution, it becomes second nature. Train for excellence so you can expect excellence. Equally important: Model excellence for your team.

Another area that must be put into every single training is leadership content. There are many types of leadership. One of the most basic types of leadership and authority is that granted simply by your position as the owner. This is basic and rudimentary at best. True leadership is demonstrated constantly and is not granted simply by position of ownership. As you progress up the leadership ladder, you will find that the best leaders actually train their teams to be leaders, thereby replacing themselves in the process. The very best leaders have trained others to train those subordinate to them to be leaders as well. This is what John Maxwell calls a level V leader, the pinnacle in leadership.

Wow, this leadership thing sounds a bit more in depth than what you thought it was, doesn't it? I'm guessing this is new to you and you didn't quite learn this in chiropractic college, right? Chiropractic colleges do not have the time to teach this; they are busy teaching people how to be doctors.

There was a period in my life when I was a lower-level leader. When you're a low-level leader, you get low-level team members and that's about it. Today, I've got incredible people on my team. These people don't have to be babysat, and they are training those who work with them to be leaders. It's amazing to watch. This is where people start to reach their God-given potentials and to create their own giant whiteboards in the sky as they accept personal responsibility for every decision they make and the consequences that result in their lives from their decisions.

Leadership must mean that you paint a broad vision of where you want your clinic to be, how you are going to get there, and, most importantly, why you want to get there. Always give your team the "why" behind the "what." Also remember that leadership and management, though not always the same, do need to be broken down in a granular fashion. A lower-level leader often chooses not to get granular and to totally ignore explaining why he wants to achieve a specific outcome or do a specific task. Higher-level leaders always focus on why instead of just what.

If you want a truly outstanding and dynamic weekly training program, train with other colleagues' offices. We do this in HealthSource all across the country in what we call pods. We have assembled training pods with groups of four to six HealthSource offices to train together. It makes for a much-higher energy event that can have much more effect than one small, isolated team attempting to train.

So, if you've got some colleagues nearby whom you could train with, I highly recommend that you do so. If you don't have any colleagues nearby, how about you get out and meet some?

This is one of the great problems in chiropractic: We tend to be isolationists and stay in our own little closed worlds and eventually wonder why the world passed us by and we are left practicing old-school methodology while the rest of the world is light-years ahead. The answer is simple: Get the heck out of your office and train with others. Stay current and stay relevant. Always provide the very best level of care possible to your patients so they achieve their health goals in an efficient and straightforward fashion.

CHAPTER 11

Insurance vs. Cash: What's the Answer?

"Success without honor is like an unflavored dish; filling but unsatisfying."

—Al Hillegass

Oh my gosh, I literally can't believe this argument is still going on today! Truth be told, both forms of rigid practices are out of date…well out of date, kind of like calling your practice a high-tech, "roller-table practice."

It seems like the argument over having a cash-based versus an insurance-based practice has been going on since it became harder to be compliant and insurance companies stopped paying out huge sums of money.

You see, in years past, especially in the 1970s and 1980s, the cash-vs.-insurance argument was absent because it was the insurance heyday.

Back then, virtually all a DC had to do was hang out a shingle and be successful financially.

Those were the decades of no- to- low deductibles and no- to- low co-pays. And to boot, benefits were extremely liberal and limitations were almost non-existent, meaning the insurance paid for nearly endless care plans with almost no out-of-pocket expenses by the patient. Documentation guidelines were rarely enforced, and care plans were not challenged for efficacy. This is why they were called the Mercedes '80s.

You know what? Because of the extremely liberal benefits, even the docs who didn't strive to provide the very best level of care were financially successful. Roller tables were everywhere to be found, stacked high with patients, as were multitudes of e-stim machines, ice packs, and hot packs. Almost all chiros were providing this level of care even though it was extremely outdated, even in the '80s. In my mind, it was a time of incredible abuse. The age of the chiropractic guru was birthed, and this merely made the landscape much, much worse as those gurus began schooling unsuspecting chiropractors in how to maximize general insurance, personal-injury (auto accident), and work-comp reimbursement instead of focusing on evolving patient care. It had terrible consequences on our great chiropractic profession—consequences we are dealing with yet today.

We had chiros prescribing endless care plans for very minor conditions and throwing on boatloads of unnecessary therapies just because they got paid to do them. It was wrong; the low point of chiropractic was reached. By the way, other types of providers were doing the same thing. Abuse was rampant.

Old-timers have told me some incredible tales of abuse and neglect. One chiropractic guru told me how he used to push on a trigger point for about 15 seconds and bill out a full unit of neuromuscular reeducation! This book is not about coding, so I'll not go into the fraud of that act (even though I'd love to). Almost every patient's insurance company got billed by that office for a unit of neuromuscular reeducation even though it wasn't even done. This same guru told me he actually got kicked out of an insurance panel because of his abuse and he thought that was a badge of honor! It literally blows my mind. I'm not saying everyone was doing this, because that was NOT the case. Let's just say that this type of practice was fairly prevalent.

Those days had huge- volume practices seeing 300, 400, 500, 1,000, and 1,500 patient visits a week, with many of the docs performing over-prescribed treatment plans and questionable therapies with no chiropractic necessity. I've got no problem with volume practices, as long as it's done the right way. I owned four of them and loved the energy…I still love it! But volume simply for the sake of volume is wrong. Volume because new patients and wellness patients are attracted to your office is fantastic!

Also during this period, roller tables really started proliferating. In many cases, these roller tables were being billed out as mechanical traction. Mechanical traction? Are you kidding me? There is no way possible you can legally justify a roller table's useless machinations as mechanical traction. Legal opinions are everywhere stating that to be true. And you know what? We STILL have docs billing roller tables as traction. I just can't understand it. It has to change; auditors are targeting this particular pattern of abuse.

Here's a clue: Any time you bill some procedure as something else, it's illegal. Don't do it. Be ethical at all times in your treatment programs. Strive for functional improvement, and when ready, transition patients to true wellness care if you think they can benefit from it.

Hint: True wellness care is MUCH more than only an adjustment. Just an adjustment is old-school maintenance care, but it can be evolved to true wellness care. Remember, the baby boomers are turning age 65 at the clip of about 10,000 people a day, and they really want wellness care. Do you know how to provide it? Do you know what it is? Are you and your family receiving it?

If this is perplexing, it's time for you to upgrade your knowledge base. Don't feel alone. I'd fathom a guess that 75% of our profession is uncertain about what real wellness care is. That's frightening and disappointing, because people really want wellness care and chiropractors are best suited to provide this care. It's right up our ally.

Case in point: Most of the docs from the '80s and '90s find it just about impossible to make the income they used to make. Most no longer know how to compete and have a shadow of their old practices. One of the docs from the '80s and '90s who I used to know now has his practice in a tiny shoebox while he tools away, seeing a few patients while pushing back the fear that the insurance company auditors will soon request his noncompliant patient records. What a sad way to live. It does not need to be this way. It's not that hard to get compliant and to attract new patients. Just make sure it's all about what's right for the patient.

As a result of the huge payouts to doctors of all ilks, the insurance companies struck back and continue to reduce benefits today. The automotive insurance companies are doing the same thing, as benefits have been slashed to the bone. Work comp has done the same thing as well. And those chiros who are personal-injury or work-comp "mills" closed up shop or moved from state to state chasing the declining reimbursements. There really is no place left, with a small exception, to set up those types of practices anymore.

One thing I didn't touch on is that due to the current lack of knowledge on many chiros' parts concerning compliant documentation, when the DCs get audited, they are getting ripped apart. Ignorance is not a defense. If you want to be a doctor, it's time to put on your big-boy (or –girl) pants and learn how to document correctly, whether the patient is paying cash or insurance is involved. Those gurus telling DCs to "go cash" seem to have zero regard for what's best for the patient.

So, ultimately, much of the environment we practice in today was created by chiropractors from the '80s and '90s. Think about that one for a minute. We did it to ourselves!

And what's even worse is that chiros formed 'unholy alliances' with third- party payers. What I mean by this is that the chiros set up monitoring or auditing or pre-authorizing organizations to essentially strip out most of the chiropractic benefits available to the patients. This is one 'perverse' relationship.

"Why would they do this?" you ask? Simple. It's all about the money. In this case, the chiros or organizations receive money as a direct result of slashing the benefits. So here's how it goes: A patient's benefits manual says he gets 40 chiropractic visits a year. The DC has to get pre-authorization, so she contacts the pre-authorization company or intermediary between the insurance company and the doctor. The company tells the doc that she must submit a bunch of paperwork to get pre-authorized care. The company eventually authorizes five visits, which can be totally useless when trying to correct a deep-seated problem with the patient's health. The pre-authorizing company receives a fat check from the insurance company for "controlling costs." Really?

Or it could be that the chiropractic doctor-owned auditing firm now requests records from the chiropractor on a set number of patients. He receives the records, stamps them "not medically necessary," and moves on to the next set of records. The doctor then has to reimburse the insurance company the money she received earlier for those services. Oh, I forgot to tell you, he gets a percentage of money retrieved from the chiro as his compensation. This is just plain wrong, in my humble opinion.

Now you know more truth. So you're thinking, "Well, maybe I should just go cash, and to hell with the insurance companies."

More truth: The same level of documentation and compliance is legally required whether or not the patient is a cash patient, period. Digest that one for a minute.

As I stated a number of chapters ago, your practice should reflect your demographics, so if 'X' percent of your community has no chiropractic coverage, your practice should be 'X' percentage cash. If your community has 'Y' percentage insurance coverage, your practice should be the same.

Patients come to us to get well. Trying to force them into an all-cash environment for the sake of making our lives easier creates a huge obstacle to that patient getting well. Treat others the way you would like to be treated, and do things for the right reason.

This being said, if a patient has only 'X' amount of chiropractic benefits, then if chiropractically necessary, use those benefits and then transition the patient to cash if they are not functionally well.

And this is very important: All wellness care is cash based. Insurance companies in most cases do NOT pay for wellness care, so it is the patient's responsibility. If you provide superior service in your community and know how to communicate the value of wellness care, it is not a challenge. Those DCs who do not provide superior service or who have not mastered the art of communication will find this a highly difficult hurdle, and that's a shame, because wellness care is what our great country needs in a bad way.

CHAPTER 12

The Look

"You can be pleased with nothing when you are not pleased with yourself."

—Lady Mary Wortley Montagu

D o you mean to tell me that the look of the office is important as well? You bet it is. In fact, it's extremely important, but it's a detail often overlooked in chiropractic.

When the patient enters your office, their eyes scan from left to right, carefully taking in the environment and ambience. What they see instantly is registered in their brain, and a first impression is obtained even before they meet you. We all do this. It's human nature. How does your office stack up? You may want to get an unbiased opinion on this. And I recommend it. No, you can't ask your mom!

So, whether it's the impression is right or wrong, your new patient fairly instantly decides whether or not this is the office for them about 10 seconds after entering your office. What they see and don't see is infinitely important. And smell, being one of the most primitive senses, is equally important.

Perhaps this discussion should best be started with a list of what instantly brands you as an iconic dinosaur readied for extinction.

How to tell if your office is terribly out of date and behind the times:

1. The patient is not greeted by an exuberant and cheerful front-desk team member.
2. The paint has lost its luster and the walls really should've been repainted three years ago.
3. The carpet has spots or is worn.
4. No flat-screen television displaying chiropractic and health related information is present anywhere in the reception room.
5. Essential supplements (private labeled, of course) are not found on modern shelves and within easy reach of the patient.
6. An antiquated sliding-glass window, also known as a sneeze guard, is present which separates your front-desk team from those patients.
7. A door separates your reception room from the rest of the office, thereby disallowing your patients to see or hear anything else in the office.
8. Non-branded posters or posters that are more than three years old litter the walls.
9. Roller tables are present.
10. More than one e-stim machine is present.
11. You can hear a pin drop because no vibrant music is being played.
12. A giant protractor leans against a wall somewhere.
13. A room dedicated only to exams is present.
14. A room dedicated only to report of findings is present.
15. An open adjusting room is present.

16. No physio balls can be found anywhere.
17. No bands or tubes are present in the rehab or exercise room.
18. No mats are present in the wellness room for functional stretching and functional exercise.
19. Deep-tissue tools are conspicuously absent.
20. The lights are turned down low.
21. No clinic-branded pamphlets can be found anywhere.
22. Old-school muscle gel is located in the adjusting rooms.
23. The owner-doctor is working with patients in the wellness room.
24. Electronic chiropractic records are nowhere to be found. Stacks of paper files are loaded into old-school file racks.
25. The phone rings and no one shouts, "new patient!" Okay, well, I love this one, and it really ramps up the energy.
26. No gourmet tea bar is anywhere to be seen.

This, of course, is only a partial list, but understand this: I've been in hundreds and hundreds of offices all across America, and the above list is a telltale sign that the office is providing outdated old-school services and treatment to patients and is therefore woefully antiquated. How did you stack up? Guess what? You can fix all the deficiencies fairly quickly, so get busy!

The office of today should be modern, clean, and highly functional. I teach that it's all about the highest and best use of every square inch of the office. Nothing should be wasted. Nothing should be superfluous. Nothing should be old-school.

Your patients' senses dictate their perceptions and therefore their realities. What they see, smell, hear, and touch instantly conveys to them whether this is the office for them, whether this is where they will receive true healing, and whether this is where they will refer their family and friends.

I'm asked all the time about the open-adjusting concept. This is a concept held over from the '80s and '90s. Once again, it's all about the doctor. An open-adjusting office is old school and essentially puts the doctor on a stage where they are essentially performing for their audience of patients sitting in the hot seats waiting to be adjusted next. Hot seats in and of themselves are also an antiquated system. It is a fun system, for sure. It's also high energy. It also creates a completely personality-dependent office from which the doctor can't escape.

An open-adjusting concept virtually guarantees that the doctor is a slave to the office and does not allow the doctor to plug in and plug out at will. It is also not a replicable system. It is firmly implanted in a personality-dependent practice. And remember, a personality-dependent practice also guarantees that the doctor will have no autonomy in life and in practice.

What is autonomy, you ask? It's basically you being able to have a life of freedom. It's you doing what you choose to do, when you choose to do it, choosing whom you want to do it with, and if you want to do it at all. It's about having a life.

I'd been chained at one point in my life. I was averaging about 175 patient visits a day in two adjusting rooms with the doors always open. Everything depended upon me and my personality always being present in the office, stoking the fire. I had a very poorly trained associate (my fault) who could not allow me any personal freedom whatsoever because the office was not running on systems. The office was running on my personality only.

Yes, the office was extremely financially successful, but the day I woke up and realized I was not even able to participate in my family's lives was the day I knew something was horrifically wrong. And I was doing everything my guru coaches were teaching me to do. The light bulb went on, and I realized the evolution had to occur if I was to get a life and achieve my dreams and not simply die one day in the adjusting room, falling over onto a patient as I checked out permanently. Yep, that's not the way I want to go.

Maybe you want to die in the adjusting room, but I sure as hell don't!

So if you don't have an open-adjusting concept, how is the office supposed to be organized? One word: functionally.

In all actuality, the adjusting rooms should ideally be located to the rear of the office, which is where the owner-chiropractor should spend 98% of her time. The chiropractor should never have to scurry up to the front desk, look over the CA's shoulder, and peer at the schedule to see "what's going on." The doctor stays in the rear of the office, doing what they do best, which is examining patients, designing detailed and personalized treatment programs, and performing modern, state-of-the-art chiropractic care and communicating with their patients. The doctor does not perform therapy in the rehab room. That would not be the highest and best use of their time and talents.

So what is a rehab room? Well, let me put it this way: At six o'clock this morning, I was walking into our local YMCA, which is a very high-tech evolution of what used to be called a gym. **Today** was "legs" day, and as I was taking off my outer shirt and stuffing it into a locker, I noticed there was a sign posted at the entrance of the workout portion of the facility. It stated "wellness area." And in their wellness area, machines, free weights, and other lifting apparatuses, all of which were the most modern and the most beneficial pieces of equipment available, were functionally placed for maximum efficiency and maximum benefit. It's a beautiful room designed for outstanding results in minimum time. In effect, it's all about "wellness." A rehab room in your office should be a microcosm of that idea, minus the expensive equipment.

For whatever reason, I found myself thinking about the title of that workout room during my leg workout. I was thinking about how a chiropractic rehab room has so many similarities with their wellness area. Remember, it's about peak efficiency and peak results in a minimum amount of time. Speaking of which, today's leg routine took only 20 minutes and comprised only five sets of exercises. Now is not the time to go into the specific science and procedural methodology of this type of workout, but suffice it to say that this workout was scientifically designed to produce maximum benefit in minimum time. It's how I approach my life. It's how HealthSource is designed to operate. In other words, if you work out at the gym following the old-school principle of about one hour of 12 to 20 sets, I can just about guarantee you that my 20-minute workout is generating better results than your 60-minute workout. In my opinion, the same can be said for how HealthSource generates hugely effective results with our patients.

So, in a HealthSource rehab room, which is located just adjacent to the reception area and can be easily viewed by patients within the reception area as well as by the front desk CAs, the magic of functional wellness occurs throughout the entire day.

This is where the functional deep-tissue, functional stretching, and functional exercise takes place. With some hyper-acute patients, passive modalities may be utilized for a very short period of time. Otherwise, it's all about functional work with our patients to achieve maximum benefit in minimum time.

Many of our wellness rooms also house lower-priced spinal decompression machines for use with those patients who have spinal arthritis or disc lesions.

All in all, today's modern and functional office has a minimum of walls with a wide-open feel. There are no rooms dedicated to exams or report of findings, and adjusting rooms with doors that can close are present in the rear of the office. State-of-the-art X-ray machines are also present.

I studied under the late, great Dr. Russell Ehrhardt, DACBR. He taught me many things, but one of the most important things he shared with me was to "always X-ray the point of pain." I followed his advice during my practice and career, and I share his advice with all the doctors I encounter.

High-energy music should be felt and heard throughout the office. A gourmet tea bar should be present, featuring an assortment of green and herbal teas. Filtered water should be available in the reception room. The colors of the office should be light and bright. Full-spectrum light bulbs should shine brightly throughout the office. Fun and healthy team members who are in shape and take care of themselves religiously should be in your employ. All in all, it's essential for you and your team to produce a WOW experience for every patient on every visit. Be the very picture of health!

Ladies and gentlemen, the look, feel, and layout of your office are monumentally important and should never be overlooked. It should be ingrained in your team to be so detail oriented that no one can possibly walk by a speck of paper on the floor without bending over, picking it up, and throwing it away. Your office should be a work of art.

CHAPTER 13

The Big Secret They Don't Want You to Know

"The reasonable man adapts himself to the world; the unreasonable one persists in trying to adapt the world to himself. Therefore, all progress depends on the unreasonable man."

—George Bernard Shaw

Let me begin with a simple statement: Marketing is NOT a four-letter word. In fact, it's an endeavor that virtually every successful business engages in, and the more successful the business, the more sophisticated the marketing program becomes. Do you have a marketing calendar? What kind of marketing programs are on it? Do you have at least one marketing activity planned each and every week of the year? If not, why not? Have you ever read a book on marketing? If not, Dan Kennedy has authored a bunch of them that you may wish to consider.

Have you ever wasted your money on an overpriced Internet marketing scheme? Have you bought a CD or notebook of ads that were supposed to work and produced virtually nothing? Yep, so have I…many times, in fact.

It's time to let you in on another little secret that the social-media marketing gurus do not want you to know about. It's a simple one, at that. Here it is: Social-media marketing is by and large an enormous waste of time, talent, and resources.

If you are investing a lot of your time in posting on Facebook, tweeting on Twitter, or posting on virtually any other social-media outlet, you're absolutely wasting a great deal of your time. As I'm writing this book, the forward thinkers, the leaders in the marketing world, are pulling their dollars out of social media marketing almost entirely.

Yes, these experts have a small presence on the social media sites, even the new ones as they arise, but it's a very small presence. They know the big secret about social-media marketing and Internet marketing in general.

Are you ready to hear it? Here it goes: The marketing gurus today realize that the majority of effective marketing is actually done via direct mail. Note: Nowhere in the last sentence did I mention Internet marketing.

I am NOT saying to ignore social media. I'm saying it is not the answer to drive hundreds of new patients into your office every month. It can certainly bring some patients in, but not a boatload. Do some social-media marketing, but save resources for more effective marketing, too. You want LOTS of marketing poles in the water, all attracting new patients from multiple sources.

So what's your best source of new patients? This one is very simple to answer: referrals! Referred new patients are always your best new patients. Let's face it, your existing patient has already told them exactly what to expect, and they are all in. Your job is easy…much easier than if the new patient is from some other source than a referral.

So let me ask you this: Do you have a systematized marketing program to generate an increased number of referrals for the next 12 months? What kind of programs are they? Do you simply rotate one program over and over again, or do you have new programs utilizing different marketing media throughout the entire year?

After reading the last paragraph, you of course realize that the last sentence was what you must have in your marketing calendar.

There are many types of referral marketing programs that you can design and implement to begin to boost the number of referrals that you currently receive. Many chiropractors are under the mistaken impression that all they have to do is provide excellent care and the referrals will flood in through the front door. I wish this were the case, but it most certainly is not.

It takes a concerted, systematically designed referral program to generate not only satisfactory numbers of referrals but also huge numbers of referral new patients each every month. I contend that every practice out there should generate at least 50 referral new patients a month. You read that right: 50.

The best way to generate more referred new patients is by producing a WOW experience for every patient on every visit. This means that you exceed their expectations each and every time they set foot in your clinic. If you simply get them out of pain and restore function, you may think you've won. You have not won. All you have done is met their expectations. Patients who have their expectations met by and large do not refer in new patients to you. Patients whose expectations are exceeded refer in new patients. What are you doing to exceed their expectations on each and every visit?

My gosh, this topic could take us several books to adequately cover. This is one of those topics that we spend hours on in our training program because it is so vitally important to your patients, to you, and to your family. Let's face it: This topic encompasses virtually everything that takes place inside and outside of your practice every minute of the day, so for purposes of this discussion, we're going to confine ourselves to specific marketing programs and procedures, because virtually everything I've covered in this book thus far pertains to increasing the number of referral new patients that you receive.

Marketing experts today contend that every month that your non-active patients do not hear from you, the value of them to your practice is reduced by roughly 10%. You may wish to reread that last sentence, because chances are you are violating it and losing the value of your non-active patient database at a burning pace. In other words, you must contact your inactive patients every single month. My suggestion is that you contact them with a reactivation marketing piece so they are even more motivated to return to your practice when necessary.

At HealthSource, every 60 days, we have a targeted direct-mail or e-mail reactivation marketing program to reactivate those patients who could derive benefit from chiropractic care. In addition, all active and inactive patients also receive a highly informative newsletter every month without fail.

As a matter of fact, most practices are failing miserably by not contacting their patients every single month. The easiest way to contact your patients every month is with a direct-mail newsletter written by you (or in our case, by HealthSource) so it does not have an off-the-shelf feel to it like all purchased newsletters. Now I know at this point you're going to be tempted to say, "Hey, this is cool; I'll just e-mail them a newsletter every month." Wrong.

If you are under the mistaken impression that you can e-mail things to your patients and they actually read them, you're delusional! It doesn't work that way. That magic "delete" button is just too easy to press. This doesn't mean that it's always a waste of time to contact your patients via e-mail, but if you think your patients are going to read an e-mail newsletter, you are sadly mistaken, regardless of what the self-declared marketing gurus tell you. Remember, those gurus make their living as a direct and proximate result of you buying their stuff, and one-size-fits-all marketing is mostly useless and a waste of money.

Your reactivation campaigns should be engaging and interesting enough so your patients will actually open the mail, touch it and feel it. As often as possible, your mailings should be three-dimensional, meaning the mail is "lumpy."

The newsletters should also be engaging and informative and should not revolve around chiropractic care. It's absolutely fine to throw in some phenomenal tidbits about chiropractic care here and there, but the newsletter should be about health with some non-health tidbits thrown in. Think *People* magazine.

People magazine is one of the most widely read publications in the world today. You can just about read one of its articles in a single session while sitting on the toilet. Your newsletter should be modeled in a similar fashion. It should have small articles on highly interesting health topics that the general public finds palatable and amusing. There should always be a call to action to help stimulate a reactivation or referral, as well. Do not—I repeat—do not buy an off-the-shelf newsletter from someone who says that newsletter is going to quadruple your new patients in three days. These people are a dime a dozen and should be dismissed fairly readily in most cases. They have a defined interest in you buying their box of stuff.

Here's a quick summary of what we've talked about so far: Your patients should receive a custom newsletter every month, and this should go to all your patients, both active and inactive. Your inactive patients should also receive a reactivation piece every 60 days in addition to the newsletters. What's an inactive patient? It's any patient in your database who has not been in your office in the past 90 days. Got it?

Other marketing campaigns to stimulate referrals are just about limitless. Patient-appreciation days are a must at least once a year. They are not hard to do and can be extremely successful once you know the recipe. Put these on the marketing calendar as well.

You should also have a no- to low-cost internal marketing campaign every month inside your office to stimulate referrals. These should be fun and high energy and should be embraced by the entire team.

Let's move on to overall marketing programs in general. To start with, here is the order from worst to best as it pertains to the ability of a marketing program to effectively generate new patients in your clinic. The order is: Internet marketing (including social media), television, radio, spinal screenings, printed marketing, direct-mail marketing, targeted direct-mail marketing.

Give that some thought and think about what it is you are currently utilizing in your marketing programs. Make adjustments as necessary, especially if you're one of the doctors out there that thinks that Internet marketing is the end-all and be-all to generating new patients. As a matter fact, even Google is now generating the bulk of their revenue from direct-mail marketing rather than Internet marketing. That blows your mind, doesn't it?

So now you know that a marketing calendar is an absolute must if you are going to increase the number of new patients walking across the threshold into your office. I stated earlier that every office should be able to achieve 50 referral new patients a month. I also believe that every office should be able to achieve 50 marketing new patients a month. Certainly, you've done the math and now realize that I think that every office should generate at least 100 new patients a month. If you think this is ludicrous, it's time for you to reconsider what you're doing wrong, because having this many new patients per month is very possible!

So, what is a marketing calendar? Come on, now, you know the answer. It's simply an enlarged calendar that you can print and hang up. On it, day by day, week by week, and month by month, you have meticulously listed out each and every marketing program, both internal and external, that you and your team will be running for the next quarter. The calendar should be done at least one quarter in advance.

I know what you're thinking at this point. You're thinking, "Tom-shack, you're an idiot. I have no time for this craziness. I'm taking care of patients all day and there is no time for me to do marketing."

First of all, unless you're seeing an absolute boatload of patients, you have the time. You are just highly inefficient and your day needs to be systematized to the minute so you can achieve peak efficiency all day every day. Truth be told, I get more done by 11 AM than most people get done in two days. This is possible only because of the peak-efficiency methods I use. I'm using one of them as I write this book and am therefore able to write about five times faster than most authors. This needs to be applied to your day, as well. This is an entirely different topic than that which is germane to this chapter. Actually, a whole book could be written just on it.

Besides, you shouldn't be the one, if you're the owner of the clinic, doing all the marketing. All you should be doing is establishing a marketing calendar. Your team should be carrying out all of the marketing activities with you participating at a low level. Now, if your team is not highly trained, as we talked about earlier in this book, it'll never happen, and you know it and I know it. That's a shame, because it's preventing you from extreme success. It's also preventing you from reaching many, many more people in your community who need chiropractic and thereby from changing lives and improving the quality of lives. It's an absolute shame.

When delegating each individual marketing activity to a member on your team, make one person the lead or point person for that activity. That person will then report to you the status of successfully completing the activity at each and every Tuesday training. If they are not held accountable, the project will die. Do not delegate into a black hole. Make sure that you notate exactly who is responsible for what and the status of the marketing project so that you always know how everyone and every activity is performing.

Marketing should never stop, regardless of outside circumstances. It's a common misconception that, for instance, from Thanksgiving Day to New Year's Day, you shouldn't be doing any marketing because of all the holiday marketing that's bombarding people. Rubbish. If you want to be successful, you must go against the grain. You must do what other people are unwilling or refuse to do. To put it succinctly: Successful people do what unsuccessful people refuse to do. So, if other chiropractors are not marketing during this time, it's the perfect opportunity for you to market.

I hope you caught the gem in the last paragraph. To paraphrase Mark Twain, when you find yourself doing what everybody else is doing, it's time for you to pause and think. My mentors have taught me much valuable advice. One of my mentors, Bob Campana, taught me "Don't be afraid to innovate, be different. Following the herd is a sure way to mediocrity." Give that a little bit of thought. If you want to be successful, don't do what everybody else is doing. Be totally different, always.

If you truly want to eliminate the personality-dependent practice so you can have freedom and life outside of your office, the 50:50 ratio applies. This means that 50% of your new patients should come from internal activities from within your practice and 50% of your new patients should come from external marketing activities, outside your practice. This is an absolute must if you are to eliminate the personality-dependent practice and release the shackles holding you back.

Start your marketing calendar today. The ultimate success of your practice depends on it.

CHAPTER 14

Patient Outcomes Assessment: What Every Successful Practice Must Have in Place

"Courage is doing what you are afraid to do. There can be no courage unless you are scared."

—Eddie Rickenbacker

The first thing you want to know is what does POA stand for, right? POA stands for Patient Outcomes Assessment. In chiropractic, a true patient outcomes assessment has been missing forever, until now.

There have been many attempts at patient outcomes assessment but all have failed. They have failed because inter-examiner reliability was extremely poor. Some examples would include things such as surface EMG, thermography, and NCM's.

When I still owned all of my personal clinics (I do not own clinics today because it would divide my time between serving our franchise family members and my personal clinics. This cannot happen. My time must be 100% devoted to our franchise family members.) I ran tests with the dozen or so doctors I had working for me on some of these patient outcomes assessments that existed at the time. To say the results for satisfactory inter-examiner reliability were dismal would be a huge understatement. The inter-examiner reliability was horrific.

So I trashed those patient outcomes assessments and began the odyssey of trying to find something infinitely better. A true patient outcomes assessment independent of the examiner did not come into being until 2013, as I am writing this chapter. I'm stoked, totally stoked.

A good friend of mine, Dr. James Chestnut, whom I've mentioned earlier, has designed a truly examiner-independent patient outcomes assessment. We now utilize this in HealthSource. The really cool thing is that you can establish an accurate baseline for your patient and then, periodically throughout the program of care, conclusively show via blood analysis exactly what your care is doing to and for the patient.

Even if you are only providing adjustments to your patients, you can still show conclusively the changes that are being made in your patients. But for those of you who have evolved your practice and now provide "real" wellness –based care to your patients, the results will blow you away, assuming the care you are providing is the correct care for each patient. It's absolutely amazing.

Part of the patient outcomes assessment pioneered by Dr. Chestnut, and now utilized by HealthSource clinics, is based on allostatic load. Allostatic load measures the effects of the patient's stress on their body by measuring specific markers in their blood. You can fairly accurately predict the patient's probability of contracting an acute or chronic disease in the next three to five years by analyzing these markers. You can watch these markers reduce when the correct care is given to each individual patient. The old-school one-size-fits-all care program that some doctors use in an attempt to build their practices fails miserably when finally put to this test.

As a matter fact, it's a clarion call to upgrade the level of care you provide to your patients. It's a wake-up call programmed directly into your head that mandates you provide the very best care to your patients on every visit.

Earlier in this book, I showed you step by step what is proven to be the absolute best care today. What is best today will be obsolete tomorrow. We must constantly strive to provide the absolute best care to our patients at all times. To merely prescribe the same kind of care to every patient who walks into your clinic is not only unethical but tantamount to malpractice. Is that your current legacy? If so, then change it! Start today. Reread the chapters of the book that specifically deal with patient care, and begin to evolve what you do in your practice with your patients. Having an objective patient outcomes assessment is mandatory.

Dr. Chestnut is one of the most forward thinkers on the planet. He is a scientist and a chiropractor, and I count him as a very good friend. I encourage you to visit his website at http://www.thewellnesspractice.com/ and begin to learn more about patient outcomes assessments.

Let me be perfectly clear: I am not telling you to begin drawing blood in your office. Labs are located all over America just for this purpose. It would be a tremendous waste of not only your time but also your resources and floor space to provide this service. The labs can do it better and more cheaply.

Some of you may be thinking, "Well, it's been a long time since school. I don't remember jack about analyzing blood results." Hey, that's okay, too, because when you use a program such as Dr. Chestnut's, the results are sent to his office first, where they are interpreted, and then the results and subsequent interpretation are forwarded to you directly. How much easier can it be?

Then there are some of you who are thinking, "Well, I'm a straight chiropractor, and I don't think blood analysis belongs in chiropractic." All I can tell you is to go ahead and stay in the dark ages. Rest assured that Dr. B. J. Palmer was on a burning quest to prove the efficacy of chiropractic care. He and his team invented numerous devices in an attempt to measure and quantify the results of chiropractic care. As a matter of fact, B. J. had a blood-analysis lab right there at his clinic! I'm confident—100% confident—that he would embrace both allostatic-load measurement and patient outcomes assessments. It's what he stood for.

I can think of only one valid reason why you would not embrace this technology, and that would be because you are afraid that your patients would not exhibit substantive changes on repeat analysis, which would indicate that your care is not making the changes that are possible. And you know what? That's okay, too, up until this minute. Now that you have been given the information on how this is possible, the onus rests upon your shoulders. You can either ignore what you have learned thus far in this book, pull the shades down low in the office, and go hide in the corner, or you can choose to become a better person, a better doctor, and a better leader and move forward. I challenge you to begin today, because you CAN do it!

In addition to a patient outcomes assessment, you must also incorporate a functional outcomes assessment into your examination process in your pre-care, active-care, and post-care process.

What is a functional outcomes assessment? You know this. One example is range of motion. When it comes to range of motion, I'm certainly not talking about those ridiculous-looking giant protractors that can unexplainably still be bought today. Seriously? How is the inter-examiner reliability utilizing that thing? Can you say "horrible"? If you've got one lurking in your office, please, throw it away today.

When we talk about range of motion, we're talking about electronic range of motion, the type of measurement that has outstanding inter-examiner reliability. Every patient who walks in your door should have range of motion measured on day one, during every reexamination, and at the conclusion of their active care program. Once the patient enters wellness care, it's really not necessary, but up until that point, it's infinitely necessary.

Not only is it necessary to demonstrate to you how the patient is progressing so that you can upgrade or alter the patient's care plan when necessary, but it is also extremely important for the patient to know exactly how they are progressing.

And not to mention that the third-party payers and courts of law also demand objective outcomes assessment and range of motion is well regarded in achieving this goal. So what should your goal be regarding range of motion? That's another softball question. Your ideal goal should be to functionally restore range of motion with every patient. This means to get their range of motion back within the normative ranges. Of course, some patients will physiologically be unable to get back within the normative ranges, but the far majority of your patients should be able to achieve that objective.

Patients can achieve that objective if and only if you are providing the correct care for them. Remember, a one-size-fits-all chiropractic treatment program is, in my mind, malpractice. I hope by now, after reading the preceding chapters, you would agree. If not, perhaps you should go back and reread the book, and this time, please be open to receiving the message, just like Aristotle stated so many years ago.

Some of you busier doctors are already thinking, "I really don't have time for range of motion. I'm too busy seeing my patients." Good for you. My goal for everybody reading this book is that you all live the truth of that statement. That would be a wonderful world. That would mean that so many more people are receiving the incredible benefits of beautiful chiropractic care. So what's the answer?

In the HealthSource model, our doctors do not perform range of motion unless it is required by state board regulation or by a particular third-party payer. We have team members who are thoroughly trained correctly to perform this simple measurement. It is done and tabulated for the doctor prior to the re-examination.

Back in the day, chiropractors were charging insane amounts of money to perform simple range of motion. I'm talking about $100, $200, $300, and $400 to perform this basic service. It was criminal. Highly unethical gurus were teaching chiropractors to do it this way and to utilize incorrect coding procedures to get paid by some insurance companies. It's a classic example of avarice. Thankfully, many of those gurus have left our profession in the past several years.

After carefully reading the CPT codes, I believe that electronic range of motion is part and parcel to a re-examination process and is not eligible to be billed for separately. Do not fall into the trap of non-compliant billing procedures, because you will eventually pay the piper and it will be expensive and stressful.

As I stated earlier, there are many claims of "build your practice and make more money by using our new widget!" Such claims go on to state that this or that new magic widget will communicate the value of your care to your patient. This should make you laugh. It does not make me laugh, however, because some unsuspecting chiropractors fall for this outlandish marketing.

The way to truly communicate the value of your care to your patients is twofold. First, the patient must get out of pain while achieving normative functional outcomes. Second, a patient outcomes assessment based in real science must be used to accurately measure exactly how the patient is healing and achieving wellness at the cellular level. Doesn't that just blow your mind? Up until very recently, this was a goal that was totally unattainable, regardless of what the salespeople selling the magic widgets were or are telling you.

So, the next time you're strolling the aisle at a chiropractic convention and a salesperson confronts you and tells you that their magic, shiny gizmo will communicate to your patients the value of your care, ask to see the science. Ask about inter-examiner reliability. Ask about what this shiny magic gizmo costs. I assure you, it will be crazy expensive. You do not need any of this stuff to build your practice. What you do need is incredible care programs and patient outcomes assessments in addition to functional outcomes assessments to track your patients' progress toward wellness. And you must become a student of communication.

All in all, simply practice with truth and honesty and combine that with the very best care available, and you can't be stopped in achieving your dreams. You can't be stopped in building your practice. You can't be stopped in changing the wellness level of your community. In other words, you will become the go-to doctor in your community for real wellness-based care. Is that the legacy you would like to leave behind? If so, it's time to get to work!

CHAPTER 15

Your Clinic's Unbridled Report of Findings

"There are two pains: discipline and regret. And if you give in to the pain of discipline, you will incur the more severe pain of regret.

Choose discipline".

—Kevin Elko

I n classic chiropractic lingo, a report of findings is simply where you communicate with the patient exactly what is wrong with them and then you describe your recommended treatment program to eliminate the pain or the problem, restore function, and bring them to a state of wellness. Wellness is a life-long goal for all patients. Let's do a report of findings on your clinic.

Before you get all antsy, having read the book up to this point, you are by now getting a really good idea on how your clinic stacks up with the new standards of care and best practices. You've probably underlined and highlighted all sorts of information in this book already. If not, go back and reread it with highlighter in hand. As a matter of fact, that's exactly how I coach the HealthSource family to read any book of interest. Always read the book with a pen or highlighter in hand, and clearly indicate what parts of the book you would like to hold onto in your mind and to begin to implement and use correctly.

Then when you are finished with the book, go back to each underlined or highlighted section and transfer that information into a central location that can be reviewed often. I do it two ways. I put the information on 3" x 5" cards and keep them in my briefcase so I can review them periodically and ensure that the information I learned becomes a part of me. I also scan them into my computer so I have them digitally, ready for review. I suggest you do the same.

To merely read a book, think about it for a bit, and then stick it on a shelf or close the Kindle is an absolute waste of your time, because unless you are truly committed to using the information that you deem pertinent and relevant to your life from that book, the book only provided temporary entertainment or distraction. If you are disciplined enough to transfer the important information into a location that you will review periodically, the information that you read will become a part of your very essence. This is how we improve ourselves. This is how we become better people, better spouses, better parents, better chiropractors, and better leaders. This is how we can begin to establish a legacy so the world is a better place for our having been here.

So, to begin your clinic's report of findings, it's obviously of paramount importance that you begin to systematize everything. To paraphrase Michael Gerber, he essentially said that you should build your business (chiropractic clinic) as if it were to become a franchise. If you were to build your office as if it were to be a franchise, it would force you to utilize systems so it becomes replicable to other offices. What the heck does this mean?

It means that if you systematize virtually everything that takes place in a given day inside your office—and I'm talking about everything that happens from when the light switch gets turned on in the morning to when it gets turned off in the evening—you are converting your office from a mom-and-pop-type operation to a real business. This is how you can get freedom in your life in the long run.

Systematization is a process whereby everything that is to be done for each individual process is clearly written out so there is no opportunity for ambiguous interpretation or follow-through by you or your team. This will give you peace of mind, assuming your team is continuously trained on all of the systems, so that everything is being done correctly and efficiently and for the betterment of the patient.

Here's an encapsulation of some of the most important systems that you should begin to carefully analyze and then write out the processes for complete and correct usage so your clinic begins to run like a well-oiled machine.

1. Patient care: This, of course, includes using state-of-the-art and scientifically proven chiropractic technique along with functional deep-tissue work, functional stretching, and functional therapeutic exercise to work synergistically with the chiropractic technique.

2. Interviewing, hiring, and firing: This is a total no-brainer. Your group interviews should be carefully scripted so you have all the questions in advance and know exactly how the process will flow leading to choosing the correct member for your team. The system should also discuss how to know objectively when it is time to bring on a new team member or terminate one for underperformance.

3. Team training: This was discussed in depth earlier in the book. It should be systematized so that prior to every

weekly training the entire process is planned well in advance.

4. Communication: Everybody utilizes scripts in their lives, it's just that most of those scripts are pretty bad. Communication is an art form and therefore has to be practiced and rehearsed. This is done so that you can become a master at ensuring that you communicate all the vital information to your patient that you feel they should know. This starts with the inbound phone call and never ends.

5. Special consultation: I believe that every office should hold a weekly special consultation, which is an opportunity for the chiropractor to communicate the rest of the information that they feel is integral to that patient understanding why they are in this office and what they should expect to receive as well as we do.

6. Progress exams: It is mandatory for re-examinations to occur every 30 days. This process should be totally systematized so that the exams are accomplished efficiently and nothing is missed. This is a perfect opportunity to continue patient education.

7. Objections: This one is hugely important. As Thoreau said so many years ago, most people live their lives in quiet desperation. I believe this to be true for chiropractors as well. Most chiropractors live in fear that their patients will toss out objections that they are not skilled enough to answer. My research shows there are really only about six objections. Systematize the answers to these objections so you can ethically teach your patients what they need to know so they finish their treatment programs to obtain maximum results. Everyone wins!

8. Wellness care: As I have stated many times earlier in this book, maintenance care is not wellness care. It's a component of wellness care, but that's about it. If you desire to deliver true wellness care to your patients, how you do that should be systematized completely. I don't mean that it's a one-size-fits-all approach so all patients receive the

same kind of wellness care, because that's ludicrous and just plain unethical.

9. Scheduling protocols: For your office to run efficiently, your team needs to know exactly how the scheduling system works. There should be specific times for treating patients, for seeing new patients, for doing reexaminations, for performing report of findings for specific services such as spinal decompression or weight loss and others. If you screw this up, your office experiences nonstop chaos, your blood pressure increases, you start feeling burned out, and suddenly, you don't want to be a chiropractor anymore and find yourself attending seminars on how to be a day trader.

10. Telephone procedures: More patients and prospective new patients are lost simply because your team has no clue how to skillfully communicate over the phone. Systematize and rehearse weekly.

11. Billing and collections: Systematize this in explicit steps so your office collects what is legally allowable. This is a huge black hole for many practices because chiropractors seem to think that the person working the front desk should handle this function as well. Rubbish. These tasks require distinctly different personality types, and one person cannot perform both functions effectively.

12. Coding and documentation: It's imperative that you know all about coding and legally responsible documentation. Get yourself to numerous seminars to master this topic, and then carefully write out everything to systematize it.

13. Associate-doctor training and selection: This is also hugely important. To have a 100% non-personality-dependent practice, you will need to implement this system flawlessly.

14. Multiple clinics: If your goal is to own and manage more than one clinic, you must first master steps 1–13. Then and only then can you consider going into a multiple-clinic reality. In today's heavily regulated era, it is also

mandatory that for a multiple-clinic system to be run correctly, the owner (you) must no longer be in active practice.

15. Marketing: This is all about the marketing calendar we spoke about earlier.

16. Statistical analysis: Your practice-management software must provide the very best in statistical and data gathering. For you to correctly understand what is really going on inside your office, you must know how to analyze the stats. You should own these stats, as should your entire team.

The preceding is a basic list of the most elementary systems that you must have to survive and thrive in building a non-personality dependent practice so that you have autonomy as well as financial success and also ensure that your patients are receiving the absolute best care available today.

Unfortunately, it's become apparent today that without systematization, your clinic will ultimately experience entropy and begin to shrink. That's the reality of the New Profession. The choice is yours: Evolve or shrink, because nothing stays constant for long.

There are basically two types of practices today, and there is great disparity between them. It's come down to old school versus new school. Would you like to be a beautiful and sleek tiger or a fossil of the long-extinct saber-toothed cat?

My suggestion is that you begin systematization with a total evolution of the patient care that you provide.

CHAPTER 16

The Difference Is the Difference, and It Starts with You

"Go confidently in the direction of your dreams. Live the life you've imagined."

—Henry David Thoreau

To survive and thrive in the New Economy, you must stand out. You must be better than the rest. It's Darwin's theory personified. But also please remember that you are not effectively in competition with others; you are in competition with yourself. And that competitive spirit must drive you to continuously improve everything that goes on inside your office AND inside that space between your ears. It starts with you. It starts with discipline. In the New Profession, there is no room for the faint of heart. Their practices will die, and they will be forced to go find something else to do for living.

So, I ask you, what the heck are you doing to take care of yourself right now? What kind of shape are you in? Do you work out? What are you eating? How many meals a day do you eat? Are you eating processed foods? Gluten? Dairy? Peanuts? How many servings of organic and fresh vegetables do you eat a day? Are you consuming foods comprised of the evil color white? How much green tea do you drink per day? How much sleep do you get? How much reading do you do every day? Are you listening to audiobooks? Are you reading and filling your mind with personal-development information? How much TV do you watch? How much walking do you do? Are your pets overweight? Are you overweight? Do you weigh more now than you did when you graduated high school? Are your kids overweight? Do your kids work out? Are you taking the basic essential supplements daily?

You know, I really hope that last paragraph got you to thinking about yourself and your life. If the average chiropractor spent as much time working on themselves as they did planning their next vacation, chiropractic would not have found itself in its current predicament.

I often use myself as a human guinea pig to test out new theories that I've either developed or been exposed to. I carefully gauge how I think and feel when implementing changes to my routines and daily disciplines. Then I take it a huge step further and run comprehensive blood work to really see at the cellular level what's going on as a result of the changes I've made.

As of right now, I'm in excellent health, and I've always been a bit of a health nut. I also get an objective set of eyes on the blood work that I run on myself. For this purpose, I use a local expert here in Cleveland who knows this stuff inside and out; he's a veritable encyclopedia of knowledge. This guy is a former professional bodybuilder, a mixed martial arts fighter, a medical doctor specializing in sports injury and anti-aging medicine, and 39 years old. I go to see him about every six months, which is about how often I run blood work on myself. How often do you have your blood analyzed?

In an earlier book that I co-wrote (*Freedom From Fat*) a few years ago, I went into some of this analysis and why it's pertinent to you. I will tell you that because of the plethora of innovations that are being made in healthcare and because of the rapid pace at which they are being made, the information is constantly evolving, and even though that book was written just four years ago, it is already somewhat obsolete in some of its conclusions.

Well anyways, about three months ago, at my last consultation with this expert, we sat across from each other while he held the results of my most recent blood work in his rather large hands. This guy is in incredible condition. He looks like a Greek Adonis and has about 8% body fat at most. I'd give most anything to have those biceps! So he looked up and said, "I just can't believe this. Not only am I jealous because your blood work is actually better than mine, but this is the very best blood work I've seen on any patient at any age in my entire career."

So I ask you again: What does your blood analysis reveal? If you haven't had it done in the past 6 to 12 months, it's time to get off your keister and find out just what the heck is going on inside your body. Blood work does not lie. Find out the truth and go get some current blood work done. Make sure it's comprehensive and that you are testing all the relevant biomarkers. The purpose of this book is not to go into all the new advances in blood-work analysis, but suffice it to say the advances are enormous. You must get current on this information, because what you were taught in school, even if you graduated just six months ago, is horrifically incomplete. Remember that in college you learned the basics. The good stuff, the really meaningful and effective information, comes post graduation. Never stop learning.

The difference between practices that are wildly successful and those that are mediocre or grasping to hold on is YOU. Where your current practice is today is a direct result of the decisions you have made in the past. Those decisions were a direct result of what was going on inside your head. If you are not 100% satisfied with the success of your practice today, it's time for you to do something different. To do the same thing over and over again and expect different results, as Einstein stated, is basically insanity. It all starts with you. The difference is you.

And you know what? The cool thing about our decision making is that we can change it right now, today. But the only way you can make better and more effective decisions is to alter what goes on inside your head. So if the present is a result of your past decisions, the future is a result of the decisions you are making today and onward. I challenge you to make better decisions.

I asked you earlier what your daily personal disciplines are. I've already described mine to you, but to summarize: I wake up earlier than most and accomplish more by noon than most people accomplish in two days. After I wake up, I focus on that which I'm grateful for in my life. I do this while still in bed. This focuses and sharpens my mind for the day. Then I read my goals out loud and focus on the 10 secrets of success as taught to me by one of my mentors, Bob Campana. I do this while shaving. Then I either head downstairs to my exercise room or off to the gym for weight training. The Vita-Mix comes out next, and I prepare a high-protein smoothie jam-packed with organic vegetables and gluten-free oats. Next, it's shower time. I also usually irritate the crap out of my beautiful bride, Lisa, as she's trying to get ready to join me in the office. Then it's off to the office, where we immediately have a morning huddle to reframe everybody for the day, perform our stretches, and implant much-needed personal-development skills. Then I grab some green tea and some filtered water and head straight to my desk. I consume green tea and water all day long.

I have one of those really cool desks called an Elevate Wrap that goes up and down so I can work from both a seated and standing position alternatively all day long. This improves my efficiency. It's also healthier than sitting down all day.

Once at my desk, I begin my highly structured day. Virtually every minute of the day is allocated to specific types of activities or tasks.

This is mandatory for peak efficiency. I check e-mail only twice a day at two specific times. My morning consists of "the burning 20s."

The burning 20s is a method taught to me by my mentor Robert Berkley. With timer on the desk, I work without interruption on my creative projects for 20 minutes. This is followed by a 10-minute break, which is used for meditation for the first two breaks of the morning. After the 10-minute break, a 20-minute high-intensity session is repeated. During the burning 20s, no interruptions are tolerated, and I mean zero interruptions. This goes on until noon and allows me to achieve more by noon than most achieve in one to three days. The afternoon is tightly structured to the minute for other specific activities or tasks.

Did you know that current research indicates if you are working on a project and are subsequently interrupted, it takes roughly 12 minutes for you to refocus to where you were before the interruption. This is crazy, isn't it? The lesson here is don't get interrupted. Don't allow it. Refuse to permit it into your reality.

When work is done, which is not necessarily dependent on what the clock says, I jump in the car and drive the three miles home. Then on three nights of the week, I grab my younger son, Zack, and we had off to martial arts for an intense workout. I earned my black belt 20 years ago, and at Zack's rather soft-touch urging, I started training again so we could spend some really cool time together. Then it's back home to consume a fantastic meal and spend time with my family. A half hour before bed is reserved for additional reading.

Regarding meals and food, I usually eat three meals along with two smaller meals between the three main meals. Depending on the day and if I've had two workouts that day, I'll typically have three smaller meals in addition to the three main meals. Again, I consume green tea and filtered water all day. If we are not fueled correctly, we cannot function at peak efficiency. Without peak efficiency, we achieve mediocrity. Mediocrity is for the birds. That just isn't good enough.

How do you structure your days?

The difference starts with you. You are the leader of your office. You dictate what occurs. You dictate every detail. Do your patients get a ride on the roller table with some e-stim or ultrasound and an adjustment and go on their way?

The difference starts with you. Only you can make a decision that you want to truly give your patients the very best you are capable of giving them. Only you can make a decision that will allow you to continuously bring in new and efficacious information to translate into superior patient care. Yes, it takes work. All superior results require effort and work.

Speaking of outcomes, are you ready to prove to yourself, to your patients, and to your team that the care you are providing now or committing to provide tomorrow is in fact making substantive long-term changes to your patients at the cellular level? I've already told you how to do this: patient outcomes assessment. Remember, this isn't some giant protractor used to grotesquely measure your patients' range of motion pre- and post treatment. I'm talking about blood analysis in addition to functional outcomes consisting of, at the very least, electronic range of motion. When you start this, it will blow you away! It will blow your patients away! It will blow your team away!

What are you waiting for? It's time to systematize everything I've listed for you in the preceding chapter and to get busy. You've got some work to do. You must start systematizing, systematizing, and systematizing. Write everything down in steps and checklists.

The difference is being different, and being different starts with YOU. The rules have changed dramatically in the New Profession. What used to work no longer works. It's an entirely new and evolved paradigm. I'm laying it out for you, but you have to do the work. But first, you must be committed. You must be disciplined, and you must be determined.

CHAPTER 17

It's Go Time!

"No problem can be solved from the same level of consciousness that created it."

—Albert Einstein

Man, oh man, have we covered some material in this book! I suspect that you are probably both excited and anxious simultaneously. You may also be overwhelmed, and that's okay. Chiropractic college taught you how to be a great clinician utilizing the methodology that was state of the art about 10 years before you graduated. The problem is that by graduation day, you were already obsolete. You just didn't know it. As a matter of fact, you thought you were one damn good chiropractor, didn't you? Yep, I did too!

Chiropractic college gave you the basics of how to be an outstanding doctor, and it does an excellent job at that task. As I was told by my martial arts instructor, when you get your black belt, the real learning starts. The same holds true for earning your chiropractic degree.

I've told you it's entirely up to you if you want to be the best. Who wants to be lying on their deathbeds, wishing they would've done better jobs, wishing they would've lived better lives, wishing they would've been more successful? Not me!

The very basic rules of thriving in practice have changed overwhelmingly. You MUST NOT ignore these changes. Importantly, you now know what these changes are, and most importantly, you now know what you must do to take charged of your practice and your life. Your future depends on taking this action.

The New Profession demands that you evolve your thinking and your patient care to be successful in today's environment. It's not that people are any more intelligent than they were in the old economy; it's just that the ease with which information flows has increased at a tremendous pace, so now your patients and prospective patients can, at the touch of a few buttons, quickly search the Web and find out what works today to help them with their current problems. If you are not utilizing what works best, you will quickly be exposed as a relic set out in a graveyard to gradually rust away into the dirt.

Running a chiropractic clinic is much more complex and infinitely more difficult than it was just five years ago. Only the committed will thrive. The doctors from the Mercedes '80s and the easy '90s are dropping like flies. It's not that these doctors are not intelligent but that they became accustomed to the gravy train of easy money and easy patients. And once people get accustomed to living on the gravy train, it's damn difficult to get them motivated or teach them how to become motivated to do what it takes to succeed. Most of these docs have faded or will fade into obscurity. Don't let this happen to you.

Systematize everything in your clinic. Write it down. Begin training with your team at least three hours a week to train for success. If you are not committed to doing this, I really don't know what to tell you, because the outlook for you is grim. If you are disciplined and committed, your outlook is absolutely fantastic! In the New Profession, you can build wildly successful practices, just by a different set of rules.

Go ahead and read this entire book again. Take notes and use a high-lighter. Read chapter 15 again, meticulously going through all of the systems I described to you. Take your time. Get it right. Get some help. Design and implement comprehensive steps for the outstanding implementation of every system mentioned.

To tell you the truth, before you do anything businesswise you learned in this book, you should begin to work on yourself first. Go back and reread chapter 16. Get some comprehensive blood work done on yourself. Make sure you check your key hormone levels—all of them—in this analysis. This is a subject for another book I may write, but if your hormone levels are off, you're fighting a losing battle. There is new literature—I'm talking brand-new—expounding on this topic. The literature also shows you how to naturally rebalance your hormones so your body is running at peak efficiency, like it did when you when you were 18 or 20 years old. Since I rebalanced my hormones, my workload, output, and efficiency have increased to record levels. Get some blood work done now!

Pay special attention to the daily disciplines that you are going to implement into your life starting tomorrow. Dismiss the BS about starting next week. Procrastination is a tool not only of the devil but also of the mediocre masses. Get it out of your life today. No one is perfect; I fight procrastination from time to time, as well. Your daily disciplines, once you're committed to them, are your ticket to rooting out procrastination, stomping on it, and heading for your dreams.

You're probably going to need help, and that's okay. I encourage you to seek out mentors, real mentors. Stay away from the outdated gurus and coaches. They mean well, but their tools are old. In my business career, mentors have played an instrumental role in helping me reach higher and higher levels of success. I also belong to mastermind groups, to which I attribute a great deal of HealthSource's innovation and resultant growth and dominance in the chiropractic industry.

When choosing mentors, choose very carefully. Avoid like the plague those who are deeply rooted in the past, because old school does not work in chiropractic anymore. You must look for innovators and leaders in the New Profession. Seek the best.

But before you move on to that step, I'm of the opinion that you need to know what it is that you want to accomplish in your life. You need to carefully sketch out your legacy. A phenomenal exercise in helping you do this is to write out your obituary. What does it say? What did you accomplish? More importantly, how were lives changed and improved as a direct result of your influence on others? Did you leave the world a better place with your existence? Or were you merely a consumer, interested in only yourself and your hedonistic pursuits? Give this one a little bit of thought. Heck, give it a lot of thought.

So, as you're thinking about what you want to do with the rest of your life, give John Maxwell's words on *what habitual winners do daily* some serious thought:

1. Winners are passionate about what they do.
2. Winners value the process of winning.
3. Winners focus on their strengths and not their weaknesses.
4. Winners focus on winning on the inside more than on the outside.
5. Winners persist on their path toward success.

Everybody wants to be a winner, don't you think? But, as coach Bear Bryant stated so many years ago, "It's not the will to win that matters; everyone has that. It's the will to prepare to win that matters."

Do you have the dogged determination to firmly implant and entrench daily disciplines in your life to put you on the path toward winning and success?

Here's another somber truth: Most chiropractors aren't equipped to undertake this mission alone in today's New Profession. Let's face it: it's a ton more complicated than it used to be. If you want to be a winner, you must surround yourself with winners and like-minded individuals on a quest for success. This is where HealthSource shines brightly. HealthSource is the world's largest chiropractic franchise family, specializing in the relentless pursuit of exceptional care, ultimately resulting in real wellness care for our patients. Doctors content with using roller tables, electrical stimulation, and ultrasound need not apply for membership in our exclusive family.

We have carefully designed, tested, and put in step-by-step recipe-like formulae: the solutions to every one of the systems you read about earlier. It's all done. There is no guesswork. The experts are assembled and stand ready to help you achieve your vision, your dreams, and your life's mission. We'll also educate you on compliance so you can practice with certainty.

At first blush, some people are put off by the term "franchise" simply because they don't truly understand what it means and stands for. Many of the most successful businesses in America today are franchises, especially in the service sector, to which chiropractic belongs. Having a franchise does not mean your practice is no longer yours. Quite the contrary, it is always your practice. No one tells you what you must do with your patients. Our job is to simply educate you on what is working the very best today to get your patients out of pain and get them functionally restored and on the road to a program of real wellness care. The ultimate decision of what you do with your patients is always up to you. Our job is to teach and help you implement the systems that can lead to ultimate freedom for you.

You can try to go it alone, and some of you may succeed while some will not. Many of you will flounder, and entropy will set in and you will reverse engines and remain where you are or slide backward. Nothing remains constant. You are either growing or shrinking. Please, choose growth. Our profession depends on it!

Most chiropractors have seen their clinics slip significantly in the last five years. And those doctors launching new practices are encountering obstacles never before seen in our profession. It seems as soon as they open, they close six months later, the doctor being relegated to "associate jail" status.

So you can stay out there and let the doctor down the street become a member of our exclusive family, supported by our family- THE owner of the HealthSource practice in your community. You can continue to go it alone in an increasingly complex, competitive, challenging, and even dangerous healthcare- business environment. Or you can continue to look at *THEM,* the consultant/guru industry, to sell you more things and kits and binders and DVDs in the false hope of building your practice.

Or you can decide to fully and thoroughly investigate everything that is involved with becoming part of the HealthSource family in your community.

You have three straightforward and simple options for how to learn more:

1. You can go to www.newchiropracticpractice.com. Watch the five-minute video "Enough Already!" Then download the 20-page report titled "Do You Have a Business or Job or Trap or Ticking Time Bomb?!"
2. You can call 1-800-250-7082 and leave your name and address, and we'll snail-mail you the report.
3. You can call the HealthSource corporate office at 1-888-967-5458 and just tell us you finished this book and that you demand some information right quick.
4. Just for kicks, you can also visit our website at www.healthsourcechiro.com and click on the "franchise information" tab. While you're there, browse the site and learn more.

Regardless of whether you decide to check out the HealthSource family, at the very least, commit to investigating your options to evolve both yourself and your practice. If you don't yet have a practice, commit to learning how to launch a practice correctly well before you begin the process. Our HealthSource LaunchU division specializes in launching new clinics.

What is going to be your legacy? Will it be success or mediocrity? The choice—and it is a choice—is entirely dependent on the decisions you make now. Let's get to work!